Cooking
with the Stars

A COLLECTION
OF FAVORITE RECIPES
OF CELEBRITIES FROM
FILM, TELEVISION, MUSIC,
SPORTS, POLITICS, BUSINESS,
AND THE CULINARY ARTS

Rick Ameil

BARRON'S

All inquiries should be addressed to:
Barron's Educational Series, Inc.
250 Wireless Boulevard
Hauppauge, NY 11788
http://www.barronseduc.com

International Standard Book No. 0-7641-1114-0

Library of Congress Catalog Card No. 99-30376

Library of Congress Cataloging-in-Publication Data
  Cooking with the stars : a collection of favorite recipes of celebrities
  from film, television, music, sports, politics, business, and the culinary
  arts / compiled and edited by Rick Ameil.
      p.   cm.
    Includes index.
    ISBN 0-7641-1114-0 (pbk.)
    1. Cookery.   2. Celebrities—United States.   I. Ameil, Rick.
  TX714.C658   1999
  641.5—dc21   99-30376
                                                        CIP

Printed in Hong Kong
`9 8 7 6 5 4 3 2

Photo Credits
ABC, Inc: page 85; Bachrach: page 129; Gary Bernstein: page 45; Robert Blakeman: page 111; Buena Vista Television: pages 61, 102; Charles W. Bush: page 113; Paul Chapnick: page 97; Rick Diamond: page 32; Zoe Dominic: page 19; Roger Dong: page 50; Jonathan Exley: page 57; Todd France: page 26; Timothy Greenfield-Sanders: page 70; Hathaway: page 22; Mark Hill/TBS, Inc.: page 123; Abigail Huller: page 16; Len Irish: page 74; Jeff Katz/Paramount Pictures: page 59; Catherine Ledner: page 104; Bill Lyle: page 100; Michael McCreary: page 120; Jim McGuire: page 62; Andrew Redington/Allsport: page 98; Denis Reggie: page 77; Webster Riddick: page 54; Lesley Sajak/King World: pages 112, 128; Rick Stewart/Allsport: page 24; USA Swimming: page 44; David Vance: page 89; Warner Bros. Inc.: page 116; Timothy White/Harpo Productions, Inc.: page 130; White House Photo Collection: page 106.

About the Author:
Entrepreneur, restaurateur, and gourmet cook Rick Ameil is a sixth-generation Californian. Before embarking on a writing and publishing career, he owned and operated a highly successful restaurant in San Francisco, California. For the past 25 years, Rick has also worked in the nonprofit sector for many charitable organizations including the March of Dimes, American Cancer Society, American Red Cross, and the United States Olympic Committee. He makes his home in San Francisco.

INTRODUCTION

*W*elcome to Cooking with the Stars—a collection of favorite recipes of celebrities from film, television, music, sports, politics, business, and the culinary arts. This "cookbook of the stars" contains an eclectic collection of 134 star-studded recipes that are the personal favorites of 87 personalities. The recipes cater to a variety of tastes and are sure to impress your friends and family alike.

Cooking with the Stars has something for everyone, from First Lady Hillary Clinton's *Chocolate Chip Cookies* to Donald Trump's fabulous *Lemon Chicken* to Chef Jacques Pepin's *Pasta with Fresh Vegetable Sauce.* Make Vince Gill's fabulous *Peanut Butter Fudge.* Try Oprah Winfrey's delicious mashed potatoes or Tommy Hilfiger's lasagna. And don't miss Joan Rivers's hilarious family recipe for toast! Each recipe is easy to recreate in your own kitchen. I am sure you will enjoy them all!

Proceeds from this cookbook benefit two very special charitable organizations: the Spirit of Christmas Foundation, which is dedicated to helping people in need; and the Koroibos Foundation, which provides financial assistance to aspiring athletes.

I would like to express our sincere gratitude to all the celebrities who contributed recipes for this cookbook. We truly appreciate their support and participation.

Enjoy! And have a great time cooking with the stars!

Rick Ameil

Cooking for Two Great Causes

Proceeds from the Cooking with the Stars celebrity cookbook will benefit the Spirit of Christmas Foundation and the Koroibos Foundation, Inc. Both organizations are California charitable corporations exempt from state franchise and income tax and are organized and operated exclusively for charitable purposes under Section 501(c)(3) of the U.S. Internal Revenue Code. Contributions to the charities are tax deductible to the extent allowed by law.

Spirit of Christmas Foundation

Founded in 1996, the Spirit of Christmas Foundation is a nonsectarian, not-for-profit, voluntary organization dedicated to helping people in need. The foundation sponsors and supports programs that directly help children, families in crisis, low-income seniors, the working poor, and others.

Foundation activities include providing free Christmas trees and holiday food boxes to economically disadvantaged individuals and families; donating toys and back-to-school supplies to needy children; and awarding grants to local social service organizations serving those less fortunate.

Koroibos Foundation, Inc.

Since its founding in 1983, the Southern California Olympians' Koroibos Foundation, Inc. has provided essential financial assistance to contending Olympic hopefuls in financial need.

Koroibos is the name of the first recorded Olympic victor, an Elean, who was victorious in what is believed to be the 200-yard dash in 776 B.C. Beginning with Koroibos's victory, the Greeks started to mark time with "Olympiads," the four-year span between the celebration of the Games.

Since its inception, the Koroibos Foundation, Inc. has provided more than 90 grants to athletes from such diverse sports as canoeing and kayaking, cycling, diving, figure skating, luge, rowing, swimming, and yachting. In addition to individual grants, donations have been made to sports programs and organizations such as the Los Angeles School of Gymnastics.

★ ★ ★ ★ ★ ★ ★ ★ ★ ★ ★ ★ ★ ★ ★ ★ ★ ★ ★

In Memory of Red Skelton

Funnyman Red Skelton charmed and delighted us on television for decades with his jokes, classic comedy routines, and hilarious antics. His comic characters like Clem Kaddidlehopper, Freddie the Freeloader, San Fernando Red, and the Mean Widdle Kid brought laughter to millions throughout the world and made him one of the most-loved comedy legends of all time.

We are pleased to dedicate this edition of Cooking with the Stars to the memory of Mr. Skelton. Red contributed his favorite recipe for *Ham Hock and Lima Beans* for inclusion in this cookbook. Sadly, he passed away in September 1997.

Red, thanks for all the laughs and for making our world a happier place.

Good night and God bless.

★ COOKING WITH THE STARS

CELEBRITY CONTRIBUTORS AND THEIR FAVORITE RECIPES

★

AMY ALCOTT   GOLF CHAMPION

Rice and Artichoke Salad

6-OUNCE PACKAGE CHICKEN-FLAVORED
RICE MIX *(such as Rice-a-Roni or Farmhouse brand)*

4 GREEN ONIONS, CHOPPED

1/2 GREEN BELL PEPPER, SEEDED AND
CHOPPED

12 PIMIENTO-STUFFED OLIVES, SLICED,
OR SMALL JAR OF PIMIENTOS

2 JARS (6 OUNCES EACH) MARINATED
ARTICHOKE HEARTS

1/3 CUP MAYONNAISE

3/4 TEASPOON CURRY POWDER

1. Cook rice as directed on package, omitting butter. Cool in large bowl.

2. Add onions, green pepper, and olives.

3. Drain artichoke hearts, reserving marinade. Halve artichoke hearts.

4. Combine artichoke marinade, mayonnaise, and curry powder. Add artichoke hearts to rice mixture, toss with dressing, and chill.

Serves 6.

$\mathcal{B}$UZZ ALDRIN   ASTRONAUT

Buzz's Quick 'n Easy Chocolate Mousse

12-OUNCE PACKAGE (2 CUPS) SEMISWEET
    CHOCOLATE CHIPS
1 1/2 TEASPOONS VANILLA
PINCH OF SALT
1 1/2 CUPS WHIPPING CREAM, HEATED TO
    BOILING POINT

6 EGG YOLKS
2 EGG WHITES
WHIPPED CREAM (OPTIONAL)

1. Combine chocolate chips, vanilla, and salt in blender or food processor and mix 30 seconds.
2. Add hot cream and continue mixing 30 seconds more, or until chocolate is completely melted.
3. Add egg yolks and mix about 5 seconds. Transfer to bowl and let cool.
4. Beat egg whites until stiff peaks form. Gently fold into chocolate mixture. Transfer mousse to serving bowl, wineglasses, or individual dessert cups, cover with plastic wrap, and chill.
5. Serve mousse with whipped cream if desired.

Serves 6.

Out of This World Cajun Shrimp Creole

2 1/2 CUPS FINELY CHOPPED ONION

1 3/4 CUPS FINELY CHOPPED CELERY

1 1/2 CUPS FINELY CHOPPED BELL PEPPER

2 TEASPOONS MINCED GARLIC

1 BAY LEAF

2 TEASPOONS SALT (OPTIONAL)

1 TEASPOON WHITE PEPPER

1/2 TEASPOON BLACK PEPPER

1/2 TEASPOON CAYENNE PEPPER

2 1/2 CUPS SHRIMP STOCK *(Knorr instant fish bouillon may be substituted)*

1 TEASPOON TABASCO SAUCE

1 TEASPOON DRIED THYME

2 TEASPOONS DRIED BASIL

3 CUPS DICED TOMATOES

1 1/2 CUPS TOMATO SAUCE

2 TEASPOONS SUGAR

1/2 POUND SHELLED AND DEVEINED SHRIMP

5 CUPS COOKED LONG-GRAIN RICE

1. Spray large saucepan with nonstick cooking spray. Add onion, celery, and bell pepper and cook over medium-high heat until onion begins to brown.

2. Add garlic, bay leaf, salt, all pepper, shrimp stock, Tabasco, thyme, and basil and cook over medium heat 15 minutes.

3. Add tomatoes, tomato sauce, and sugar and simmer 30 minutes uncovered, stirring occasionally.

4. Turn heat off and add shrimp. Stir 5 minutes or until shrimp turn pink. Serve immediately over rice.

Serves 4.

To devein shrimp, hold the shrimp under a slow stream of cold water and run the tip of a knife down the back of the shrimp. Remove the "vein," the dark-colored intestinal tube running along the shrimp's back.

TIM ALLEN   ACTOR/COMEDIAN

Chicken Divan

2 10-OUNCE PACKAGES FRESH OR FROZEN
BROCCOLI, COOKED UNTIL CRISP-TENDER
8 BONELESS, SKINLESS CHICKEN BREASTS,
POACHED (DO NOT OVERCOOK)
2 CANS (10 1/2 OUNCES EACH) CONDENSED
CREAM OF CHICKEN SOUP
1 CUP MAYONNAISE

1 TEASPOON LEMON JUICE
1/8 TEASPOON CURRY POWDER
1/2 CUP SHREDDED CHEDDAR CHEESE
1/2 CUP SOFT BREAD CRUMBS
1 TABLESPOON BUTTER
STRIPS OF PIMIENTO (OPTIONAL)

1. Drain broccoli and arrange in 9 × 12-inch casserole. Slice chicken breasts and place chicken over broccoli. Preheat oven to 350°F.

2. Combine soup, mayonnaise, lemon juice, and curry powder. Spread mixture over chicken. Top with Cheddar cheese and bread crumbs. Dot with butter.

3. Bake uncovered 1 1/2 hours. Garnish with pimiento if you wish.

Serves 8.

Broccoli is available in markets year-round, but it is best from October to May. Stems should not be thick. Wilted leaves may indicate old age. Do not buy if buds are open or yellowish. Bud clusters should be firm, closed, and of good green color. Use as soon as purchased. Refrigeration will help retain the vitamin A and C content.

Swedish Meatballs

1/2 CHOPPED ONION
VEGETABLE OIL
1 1/2 POUNDS GROUND BEEF CHUCK
1/2 POUND GROUND PORK
1/2 CUP LIGHT CREAM
1/4 TO 1/2 CUP FINE, DRY BREAD CRUMBS

1 OR 2 EGGS
1/4 CUP WATER
1 1/2 TEASPOONS SALT
1/4 TEASPOON PEPPER
BUTTERED NOODLES

1. Sauté onion in a little oil until transparent.

2. Combine onion in mixing bowl with remaining ingredients. Mix well. Shape into small balls.

3. Fry meatballs in hot oil and drain on paper towels.

4. To make the gravy: Remove all but 2 teaspoons of drippings from pan. Stir in 2 tablespoons flour until smooth. Gradually add 1/2 cup light cream and 1 1/2 cups water. Bring to a boil, stirring. Season with salt and pepper to taste.

5. Add meatballs and simmer until heated through. Serve with noodles.

Serves 6.

To keep meatballs from falling apart when cooking, try refrigerating them for 20 minutes before cooking.

$\mathcal{R}$ICK AMEIL　　THE HOLLYWOOD GOURMET

Grandma Morelli's Meat Sauce

1 TABLESPOON OLIVE OIL

1 MEDIUM ONION, CHOPPED

3/4 POUND ITALIAN SAUSAGE, CASINGS
　　REMOVED

2 LARGE GARLIC CLOVES, FINELY CHOPPED

28-OUNCE CAN ITALIAN PLUM TOMATOES

16-OUNCE CAN TOMATO PUREE

1 TEASPOON DRIED BASIL

1 TEASPOON DRIED OREGANO

SALT AND PEPPER

1 POUND DRIED PASTA

FRESHLY GRATED PARMESAN CHEESE

1. Heat oil in heavy medium saucepan over medium heat. Add onion and sauté until tender, about 10 minutes. Add sausage and garlic and sauté until sausage is cooked, breaking up with fork, about 8 to 10 minutes.

2. Puree tomatoes with juice in processor. Add to saucepan with canned tomato puree, basil, and oregano. Simmer about 30 minutes, stirring occasionally. Season sauce with salt and pepper.

3. Cook pasta in large pot of boiling salted water until just tender. Drain thoroughly. Serve with sauce and top with grated Parmesan cheese.

Serves 6.

My great-grandmother Eugenia Morelli's quick and scrumptious old-fashioned recipe for pasta sauce. The sauce is great over spaghetti, penne, ravioli, or tortellini.

Mom's Pot Roast with Vegetables

4-POUND BONELESS CHUCK ROAST, ROLLED AND TIED

SALT AND PEPPER

1 TABLESPOON OLIVE OIL

2 ONIONS, FINELY CHOPPED

4 GARLIC CLOVES, FINELY CHOPPED

3/4 CUP CANNED CRUSHED TOMATOES

1/4 CUP RED WINE VINEGAR

1 TABLESPOON FIRMLY PACKED BROWN SUGAR

1 BAY LEAF

2 1/2 CUPS WATER

1 POUND CARROTS, PEELED AND CUT INTO 1-INCH-THICK SLICES

1 POUND SMALL RED POTATOES, PEELED

1 1/2 TABLESPOONS CORNSTARCH DISSOLVED IN 1 1/2 TABLESPOONS COLD WATER

1. Preheat oven to 350°F. Pat beef dry and season with salt and pepper on all sides.

2. In large, heavy flameproof casserole heat oil over medium-high heat until hot but not smoking and brown meat. Transfer beef to a plate.

3. Add onions and garlic to casserole and sauté until onions are golden. Stir in tomatoes, vinegar, brown sugar, bay leaf, and water and bring to a boil.

4. Return beef to casserole. Cover and braise beef in oven 1 hour. Add carrots, cover, and braise 30 minutes. Add potatoes, cover, and braise 30 more minutes, or until beef and vegetables are tender.

5. Using slotted spoon, transfer beef to cutting board and let stand 10 to 15 minutes. Remove carrots and potatoes from casserole and keep warm in oven. Skim fat from juices and bring to full boil. Add cornstarch mixture, stirring constantly, to thicken gravy. Simmer gravy 2 minutes. Discard bay leaf and season with salt and pepper to taste.

6. Slice beef and place on platter with carrots and potatoes. Serve gravy on the side.

Serves 4.

I love my mom's pot roast! And whenever I go home, I know if she's preparing this recipe . . . I can smell the wonderful aroma the minute I get to the front door.

Treasure Island Stuffed Rolls

2 DOZEN FRENCH ROLLS
1/4 CUP VEGETABLE OIL
1 1/2 POUNDS SHARP CHEDDAR CHEESE, GRATED
2 BUNCHES GREEN ONIONS, DICED
1 GREEN BELL PEPPER, SEEDED AND DICED
10-OUNCE CAN LAS PALMAS ENCHILADA SAUCE
1/2 CUP TOMATO SAUCE
6 HARD-BOILED EGGS, CHOPPED
1 CAN CHOPPED BLACK OLIVES
SALT AND PEPPER

1. Hollow out french rolls.

2. In large bowl, combine vegetable oil, cheese, green onions, bell pepper, enchilada sauce, tomato sauce, eggs, and olives. Season with salt and pepper to taste.

3. Preheat oven to 350°F. Stuff french rolls with filling and wrap individually in foil. Bake about 30 minutes or until heated through.

Makes 24 stuffed rolls.

Turkey Burgers

1 POUND GROUND TURKEY BREAST
1/4 CUP FINELY SHREDDED CARROT
1/4 CUP FINELY SHREDDED ZUCCHINI
1/4 CUP FINELY CHOPPED MUSHROOMS
2 TABLESPOONS DRIED ONION FLAKES
2 TABLESPOONS SOY SAUCE
4 WHOLE-WHEAT HAMBURGER BUNS, SPLIT
VEGETABLE OIL COOKING SPRAY FOR GRILL, IF NECESSARY
4 LARGE LETTUCE LEAVES
4 1/4-INCH-THICK SLICES RED ONION
4 1/2-INCH-THICK SLICES RIPE TOMATO

1. In large bowl blend turkey, carrot, zucchini, mushrooms, onion flakes, and soy sauce with hands until just combined. Chill mixture, covered, at least 1 hour and up to 4 hours for flavor to develop.

2. Prepare grill.

3. Form turkey mixture into 4 patties. Grill buns, cut side down, until golden, about 1 minute. Transfer to platter.

4. Spray grill with vegetable oil if needed. Grill patties 4 to 5 minutes on each side, or until just cooked through.

5. Make sandwiches with burgers, buns, lettuce, tomato, and onion.

Serves 4.

These rolls are delicious! Great for lunch, dinner, and parties. Bet you can't eat just one!

A great alternative to beef. These burgers are moist, tasty, and very low in fat!

JULIE ANDREWS   ACTRESS

Cottage Cheese Meatloaf

1 POUND LEAN GROUND BEEF OR VEAL	1 TABLESPOON PREPARED MUSTARD
1 CUP COTTAGE CHEESE	2 TABLESPOONS CHOPPED ONION
1 EGG	3/4 TEASPOON SALT
1/2 CUP QUICK ROLLED OATS	1/8 TEASPOON PEPPER
1/4 CUP KETCHUP	1/3 CUP GRATED PARMESAN CHEESE

1. Preheat oven to 350°F. Combine all ingredients except Parmesan cheese and mix lightly until well blended. Press mixture loosely into shallow 8-inch square baking pan.

2. Bake meatloaf uncovered 20 minutes. Remove from oven and sprinkle Parmesan cheese evenly over top. Return to oven and continue to bake 10 more minutes.

3. Let stand 5 minutes before cutting into squares.

Serves 4.

I like to double this recipe and put one in the freezer for another time!

Gratin Dauphinois

2 POUNDS BOILING POTATOES
1 LARGE GARLIC CLOVE, FINELY CHOPPED
2 1/2 CUPS MILK
1 CUP HEAVY CREAM
1/2 TO 3/4 TEASPOON SALT
1/2 TEASPOON WHITE PEPPER
1 TABLESPOON BUTTER
3/4 CUP GRATED SWISS CHEESE

1. Peel potatoes. Wash and dry thoroughly. Slice fairly thin. (Do not soak in water.) Butter 1 1/2-inch-deep baking dish.

2. Preheat oven to 350°F. Combine potato slices in large saucepan with garlic, milk, cream, salt, and pepper and bring to boil over medium heat, stirring with wooden spoon to prevent scorching. As liquid begins to heat, mixture should thicken slightly.

3. When mixture has thickened, pour into prepared baking dish. Sprinkle with grated cheese. Place baking dish on cookie sheet. Bake about 1 hour or until potatoes are nicely browned and tender when pierced with tip of knife. Let cool 15 to 20 minutes before serving.

Serves 8.

Sliced Peach Betty

2 CUPS SLICED FRESH OR FROZEN PEACHES
1 CUP PACKED BROWN SUGAR
1 CUP ALL-PURPOSE FLOUR
1/4 TEASPOON CINNAMON
1/8 TEASPOON NUTMEG
1/2 CUP (1 STICK) BUTTER

1. Preheat oven to 350°F. Place peaches in buttered baking dish.

2. Mix dry ingredients and cut in butter. Sprinkle mixture over peaches. Bake until golden, about 40 minutes.

Serves 6.

When peeling garlic, try rinsing the garlic in hot water first. The skin will come off more easily. Garlic will keep for up to 3 months if stored in a cool, dark, dry place.

To ripen fruit, place it in a brown paper bag for a few days.

ROCKY AOKI

RESTAURATEUR/BUSINESSMAN

Benihana's Fried Rice

1 CUP UNCOOKED JAPANESE RICE OR
LONG-GRAIN WHITE RICE
5 TABLESPOONS BUTTER
1 CUP CHOPPED ONION
1 CUP CHOPPED CARROT
2/3 CUP CHOPPED GREEN ONIONS
3 TABLESPOONS SESAME SEEDS
5 EGGS
5 TABLESPOONS SOY SAUCE
SALT AND PEPPER

1. Cook rice according to package directions.

2. Melt butter in large skillet. Add onion, carrot, and green onions and sauté until onion is translucent. Set aside.

3. Place sesame seeds in small skillet and toast over medium heat until golden brown, shaking pan for even color.

4. Lightly grease large skillet. Beat eggs. Pour into hot skillet and cook as you would scrambled eggs.

5. Combine rice mixture, sesame seeds, and eggs. Add soy sauce and stir. Season with salt and pepper to taste.

To obtain the right amount of water to cook rice without measuring, place a quantity of rice in a pot. Shake the pot to smooth out and settle the rice. Place your index finger lightly on top of the rice—don't make a dent in the rice—and add water until your first knuckle is covered (about 1 inch above the surface of the rice).

Benihana's Superb Salad Dressing

1/2 CUP SOYBEAN OIL
1/4 CUP RICE VINEGAR
3 TABLESPOONS TOMATO PASTE
1 TABLESPOON SOY SAUCE
1/2 TEASPOON SALT
1/2 TEASPOON GROUND GINGER
1/2 CUP THINLY SLICED CELERY
1/4 CUP COARSELY CHOPPED ONION

1. Combine all ingredients in blender and mix at medium speed 3 to 5 seconds, until celery is finely grated.

2. Add desired amount to salad and toss.

Makes about 1 1/2 cups.

*M*ATT BIONDI OLYMPIC CHAMPION — SWIMMING

Lentil Curry Soup

3 1/2 CUPS MUNG DAL, RINSED *(salmon-pink Indian lentils, found at natural food stores and Indian markets)*

10 CUPS WATER

1 TO 2 TABLESPOONS VEGETABLE OIL OR GHEE (CLARIFIED BUTTER)

1 TABLESPOON GRATED FRESH GINGER

2 TO 3 TEASPOONS TURMERIC

2 TEASPOONS CUMIN SEED

2 TEASPOONS BLACK MUSTARD SEEDS

2 TEASPOONS CRUSHED RED CHILI FLAKES

1 TEASPOON ASAFOETIDA

1 TEASPOON GROUND CORIANDER

1 TEASPOON DRIED MARJORAM

1 TEASPOON RUBBED SAGE

3 BAY LEAVES

SALT

CHOPPED CILANTRO (FRESH CORIANDER), OPTIONAL

1. Cook dal in water until tender and mushy, about 30 to 35 minutes, stirring often.

2. Heat oil or ghee in small saucepan. Add spices and stir until aromatic.

3. Add spice mixture to cooked dal. Season with salt to taste. Add more water if soup is too thick. Garnish with chopped cilantro leaves, if desired.

Asafoetida is a flavoring obtained from a large fennel-like plant that grows in India and Iran. Popular in many Indian dishes, it has a garlicky smell and should be used in very small quantities. It is available in lump or powdered form at Indian markets.

Pasta Biondi (Penne with Two Cheeses)

1 1/2 CUPS CHOPPED ONION

3 TABLESPOONS OLIVE OIL

1 TEASPOON MINCED GARLIC

3 CANS (28 OUNCES EACH) ITALIAN PLUM TOMATOES, DRAINED AND DICED

2 TEASPOONS DRIED BASIL

1 1/2 TEASPOONS CRUSHED RED PEPPER

2 CUPS LOW-SALT CHICKEN BROTH

SALT AND PEPPER

1 POUND RIGATONI OR PENNE PASTA

2 1/2 CUPS GRATED HAVARTI CHEESE

1/3 CUP PITTED, SLICED KALAMATA OLIVES OR SLICED BLACK OLIVES

1/3 CUP GRATED PARMESAN CHEESE

1/4 CUP CHOPPED FRESH BASIL

1. Sauté onion in 1 tablespoon oil until soft. Mix in garlic, tomatoes, dried basil, crushed red pepper, and chicken broth and bring to boil. Reduce heat and simmer to thick sauce, approximately 1 hour and 10 minutes. Season with salt and pepper. (Sauce can be made two days ahead; cover, chill, and warm over low heat.)

2. Preheat oven to 375°F. Cook pasta until slightly tender, but still firm. Drain pasta and toss in 2 tablespoons olive oil. Pour sauce over pasta; mix in Havarti cheese. Transfer pasta to 13 × 9 × 2-inch baking dish. Sprinkle with olives and Parmesan cheese. Bake 30 minutes. Sprinkle with fresh basil.

Serves 6.

Kalamatas are an almond-shaped Greek olive. They have a dark eggplant color and a rich, fruity flavor. Kalamatas are packed in either vinegar or olive oil and are available at most supermarkets.

ℬONNIE BLAIR   OLYMPIC CHAMPION — SPEED SKATING

Peanut Butter Cookies

1 CUP (2 STICKS) BUTTER, SOFTENED	2 EGGS
1 CUP PEANUT BUTTER	1 TABLESPOON MILK
1/2 TEASPOON SALT	2 CUPS SIFTED ALL-PURPOSE FLOUR
1 CUP SUGAR	1/2 TEASPOON BAKING SODA
1 CUP PACKED BROWN SUGAR	

1. Preheat oven to 325°F. Combine butter, peanut butter, and salt and mix well.
2. Gradually add sugar and brown sugar, and cream well after each addition. Blend in eggs and milk.
3. Sift flour and baking soda together and add to peanut butter mixture.
4. Drop by teaspoonfuls on cookie sheet. Flatten each cookie with fork. Bake until firm, 15 to 20 minutes.

Makes 2 to 3 dozen cookies.

Store crisp cookies in a cookie can with a loose cover. If they are in a tightly sealed container, they may lose their crispness.

*B*ILL BLASS   **FASHION DESIGNER**

Meatloaf

2 POUNDS CHOPPED SIRLOIN GROUND WITH 1/2 POUND VEAL AND 1/2 POUND PORK

1 CUP CHOPPED CELERY

1 CUP CHOPPED ONION

1 TABLESPOON BUTTER

1/2 CUP CHOPPED PARSLEY

1/3 CUP SOUR CREAM

1 1/2 CUPS SOFT BREAD CRUMBS

1 EGG BEATEN WITH 1 TABLESPOON WORCESTERSHIRE SAUCE

12-OUNCE BOTTLE HEINZ CHILI SAUCE

SALT AND PEPPER

PINCH EACH OF THYME AND MARJORAM

1. Preheat oven to 350°F.

2. Sauté celery and onion in butter until translucent. Add remaining ingredients (except chili sauce) and form loaf. Top with chili sauce. Bake 1 hour.

Serves 6.

Suggested
accompaniments:
Red pepper jelly
Mashed potatoes served in
*   potato shells*
Green vegetable

CHEF DANIEL BOULUD

CAFE BOULUD, NEW YORK CITY

Potato Cakes with a Chicory-chocolate Chantilly

For Dates and Vanilla Syrup:

1 1/2 CUPS WATER

1/4 CUP SUGAR

1 VANILLA BEAN, SPLIT LENGTHWISE AND
    SCRAPED, SCRAPINGS RESERVED

4 DATES, PITTED, EACH CUT INTO 8 SLIVERS

1. Combine water, sugar, vanilla bean, and scrapings in small saucepan and bring to boil.

2. When liquid boils, remove from heat.

3. Add dates and set aside to cool (can be made one day in advance, cooled completely, covered with plastic wrap, and refrigerated overnight).

For Chicory-chocolate Chantilly:

1 CUP WHIPPING CREAM (PLUS A LITTLE
    EXTRA IF NEEDED)

1 TABLESPOON GROUND ROASTED CHICORY

1/3 CUP ROASTED COFFEE BEANS, COARSELY
    CRUSHED

5 1/2 OUNCES MILK CHOCOLATE, COARSELY
    CHOPPED

1. Combine cream, chicory, and coffee in saucepan and bring to boil.

2. Place chocolate in metal mixing bowl. Remove saucepan from heat and cover. Let infuse for 15 minutes, then strain into Pyrex measuring cup.

3. Add cream if necessary to make 1 cup and transfer mixture to clean saucepan.

Return to boil and pour over chocolate. Whisk gently until mixture comes together and forms a ganache. Chill in refrigerator.

For Potato Cakes:

UNSALTED BUTTER AND FLOUR FOR PREPARING MOLDS

2 LARGE EGG WHITES

1/2 VANILLA BEAN, SPLIT LENGTHWISE AND SCRAPED, SCRAPINGS RESERVED

1/2 CUP SUGAR (PLUS EXTRA TO SPRINKLE ON TOP OF CAKES)

1 LARGE IDAHO POTATO, PEELED, BOILED, AND PUT THROUGH FOOD MILL, AT ROOM TEMPERATURE, TO MAKE 1 CUP PUREE

3 1/2 TABLESPOONS UNSALTED BUTTER, MELTED

2 TABLESPOONS WHIPPING CREAM

3 LARGE EGG YOLKS

2 TABLESPOONS ALL-PURPOSE FLOUR

1/2 TEASPOON BAKING POWDER

1 TABLESPOON PINE NUTS

1/4 CUP SLICED BLANCHED ALMONDS

1. Center rack in oven and preheat to 400°F. Butter and flour eight 3 × 1 1/2-inch ring molds and arrange on cookie sheet.

2. Combine egg whites and vanilla bean scrapings in bowl of electric mixer fitted with whisk attachment and whip at medium-low speed until foamy. Increase speed to medium-high and whip, gradually adding 2/3 of the sugar, until whites are glossy and hold firm peaks.

3. Meanwhile, whisk potato, butter, cream, and yolks in large bowl. In separate bowl, mix flour, remaining sugar, and baking powder; add to potato mixture. Gently fold whites into potato mixture using rubber spatula.

4. Fill pastry bag with mixture and pipe into prepared molds, filling approximately halfway. Sprinkle each cake with several pine nuts and generous pinch of almond slices. Bake about 12 minutes, rotating once, until cakes are golden brown, springy to touch, and pull away from sides of molds. A knife inserted into cakes should come out clean. Run a paring knife between cakes and molds and unmold. Cool on wire rack.

5. To serve, place a potato cake in the center of each of eight serving plates. Arrange date slivers in a couple of crisscrosses on the plate and garnish with an oval scoop of chicory chantilly. Drizzle vanilla syrup around potato cake.

Serves 8.

*This recipe appears in *Café Boulud Cookbook* by Daniel Boulud and Dorie Greenspan, Scribner, 1999.

$\mathcal{B}$ARBARA BUSH   FORMER FIRST LADY

Barbecued Chicken

3-POUND FRYER, QUARTERED
1 LARGE GARLIC CLOVE, CRUSHED
1 TEASPOON SALT
1/2 TEASPOON PEPPER
1 TABLESPOON VEGETABLE OIL
3 TABLESPOONS FRESH LEMON JUICE

1. Combine all ingredients except chicken in heavy zip-lock bag. Add chicken and shake to coat. Refrigerate 24 hours if possible, turning bag several times.

2. Prepare barbeque grill. When coals are ready, place chicken on grill skin side up, basting with marinade. Cook until browned before turning. (If baking in oven, bake at 400°F, skin side down first).

3. About 2 minutes before removing from heat brush with your favorite bottled barbecue sauce or my homemade version.

Serves 4.

Easy Steps to Starting a Fire in a Kettle-Type Grill

- *Open all the vents and the hood and remove the cooking grill.*
- *To get a good fire, use a high-quality hardwood charcoal or wood such as mesquite. Charcoal made from birch, elm, hickory, maple, or oak will burn clean, with no unpleasant odors.*
- *Use an easy fire-starter appliance, such as "Easy Embers," or an electric starter. Coals should burn 15 to 20 minutes, until covered with a light gray ash.*
- *Space coals 1/2 inch apart. This helps prevent flareups from drippings, as some of the drippings will fall between the coals.*

Barbecue Sauce

1/4 CUP CIDER VINEGAR
2 1/4 CUPS WATER
3/4 CUP SUGAR
1/2 CUP (1 STICK) BUTTER OR MARGARINE
1/3 CUP YELLOW MUSTARD
2 ONIONS, COARSELY CHOPPED
1/2 TEASPOON SALT
1/2 TEASPOON PEPPER
1/2 CUP WORCESTERSHIRE SAUCE
2 1/2 CUPS KETCHUP
6 TO 8 TABLESPOONS FRESH LEMON JUICE
CAYENNE PEPPER

1. Combine first eight ingredients in saucepan and bring to boil. Simmer over low heat 20 minutes or until onion is tender.

2. Add the remaining four ingredients and stir. Simmer slowly 45 minutes. Taste for seasoning. This sauce freezes well.

Makes about 8 cups.

Red, White, and Blue Cobbler

21-OUNCE CAN BLUEBERRY PIE FILLING (OR USE HOMEMADE FILLING BELOW)
21-OUNCE CAN CHERRY PIE FILLING (OR USE HOMEMADE FILLING BELOW)

1. Preheat oven to 400°F. Spread blueberry pie filling in bottom of 8 × 8-inch baking pan. Spread cherry filling on top, smoothing to edges of pan.

2. Place pan in oven to heat while preparing topping.

For Topping:

3 TABLESPOONS SHORTENING
1 CUP ALL-PURPOSE FLOUR
1 TABLESPOON SUGAR
1 1/2 TEASPOONS BAKING POWDER
1/2 TEASPOON SALT
1/2 CUP MILK

3. Cut shortening into dry ingredients until mixture forms fine crumbs. Stir in milk. Drop by spoonfuls onto hot filling.

4. Return to oven and bake 25 to 30 minutes or until browned. Serve topped with vanilla ice cream.

   Serves 6.

   The following recipes are for homemade fillings.

For Blueberry Filling:

1/2 CUP SUGAR
1 1/2 TEASPOONS CORNSTARCH
2 CUPS FRESH OR FROZEN UNSWEETENED BLUEBERRIES
1/2 TEASPOON FRESH LEMON JUICE

Mix sugar and cornstarch in saucepan. Add blueberries and lemon juice. Cook until thickened.

For Cherry Filling:

GENEROUS 1/2 CUP SUGAR
1 1/2 TABLESPOONS CORNSTARCH
11-OUNCE CAN SOUR PIE CHERRIES
1/8 TEASPOON CINNAMON
1/8 TEASPOON ALMOND EXTRACT

Mix sugar and cornstarch in saucepan. Gradually stir in juice from canned cherries and cook until thickened. Add cherries and flavorings and remove from heat.

GEORGE BUSH

FORMER PRESIDENT OF THE UNITED STATES

Black Bean Salad

15 1/4-OUNCE CAN WHOLE KERNEL CORN, DRAINED

15-OUNCE CAN BLACK BEANS, RINSED AND DRAINED

3/4 CUP CHOPPED GREEN ONIONS

1 RED BELL PEPPER, SEEDED AND CHOPPED

2 GARLIC CLOVES, MINCED

1/4 CUP CHOPPED CILANTRO

1/3 CUP COARSELY CHOPPED PECANS

1. Combine all ingredients in bowl; mix well and set aside. Prepare the dressing.

For the Dressing:

2 TABLESPOONS VEGETABLE OIL

3 TABLESPOONS FRESH LEMON JUICE

2 TABLESPOONS SOY SAUCE

1 TABLESPOON DIJON MUSTARD

2. Add all ingredients to bowl and mix well; cover and marinate overnight in refrigerator.

Serves 4 to 6.

Jimmy Carter

Former President of the United States

Roasted Wild Duck in Oven Bag

1 fresh duck (about 5 pounds)
Salt
1 apple, quartered and cored
1 tablespoon butter
1/4 cup honey
1/4 cup orange juice
1 teaspoon grated orange peel
1/4 teaspoon ground ginger
1/4 teaspoon dried basil
1 oven bag

1. Preheat oven to 375°F. Wash duck well and dry with paper towel. Salt body cavity and outside of duck and stuff cavity with apple.
2. Mix butter, honey, orange juice, orange peel, ginger, and basil and heat until butter melts.
3. Place duck in oven bag. Pour half of liquid into duck cavity and the rest over duck. Tie bag and make 6 1/2-inch slits in top of bag. Roast 1 1/2 hours or until tender.
4. Pour sauce into bowl and skim fat. Discard apple. Serve sauce with duck.

Serves 4.

No-cream Cream of Broccoli Soup

1 medium onion, chopped
1 garlic clove, crushed
1 tablespoon sunflower oil or other vegetable oil
1 bay leaf
1 pound broccoli, chopped
1 small potato
2 1/2 cups vegetable stock
Salt and pepper
Juice of 1/2 lemon
Low-fat plain yogurt *(or sour cream if you're not watching calories or cholesterol)*

1. Sauté onion and garlic in oil with bay leaf until soft, 3 to 4 minutes.
2. Add broccoli, potato, and stock. Cover and simmer gently 10 minutes. (Broccoli should be tender but still bright green.) Remove bay leaf and let soup cool a little.
3. Puree soup in blender, but not until completely smooth. Season to taste. Add lemon juice. Reheat if necessary. Add a dollop of yogurt just before serving.

Serves 4.

★ ★ ★ ★ ★ ★ ★ ★ ★ ★ ★ ★ ★ ★ ★ ★ ★ ★ ★

Dick Clark ENTERTAINMENT EXECUTIVE

Cajun Corn Chowder

2 1/4 CUPS NONFAT MILK

14 1/2-OUNCE CAN CHICKEN BROTH

1 CUP FROZEN CORN

10 1/2-OUNCE CAN GREEN GIANT MEXICORN

7 1/4-OUNCE JAR ROASTED PEPPERS,
    DRAINED AND CHOPPED

1 CUP CHOPPED ONION

1 CUP CHOPPED CELERY

2 TABLESPOONS BUTTER OR MARGARINE

Season the chowder with the following spices to your own taste:

CELERY SEED

CAYENNE PEPPER

PAPRIKA

GARLIC POWDER

ONION POWDER

COARSELY GROUND BLACK PEPPER

MARJORAM

BEAU MONDE SEASONING

1. Combine milk, chicken broth, frozen corn, canned Mexicorn, and roasted peppers in large saucepan. Add selected spices.

2. Sauté onion and celery in butter until tender. Add to soup and simmer 10 to 15 minutes. Let stand 1 to 2 hours. Reheat and serve.

Serves 6.

KATHY JOHNSON CLARKE

OLYMPIC CHAMPION — GYMNASTICS

Spinach Salad

2 BUNCHES FRESH SPINACH

1/4 CUP WINE VINEGAR

1/2 CUP SUGAR

1/4 TEASPOON PAPRIKA

1 TEASPOON SALT

1/4 CUP VEGETABLE OIL

1 TABLESPOON CHOPPED RED ONION

1 TABLESPOON TOASTED SESAME SEEDS

3 TABLESPOONS BACON BITS

2 HARD-BOILED EGGS, CHOPPED

CROUTONS (OPTIONAL)

RAISINS (OPTIONAL)

1. Clean spinach and place in large salad bowl. Combine vinegar, sugar, paprika, and salt in small saucepan and bring to boil. Mix vinegar mixture with oil, onion, and sesame seeds.

2. Toss salad with bacon bits and egg, then with dressing.

Serves 8.

For a more tangy dressing that is also lower in fat, use 1/2 cup vinegar and reduce oil to 2 tablespoons. Use olive oil for a great source of healthful monounsaturated fats. You may also use 4 hard-boiled egg whites instead of the entire egg.

ℋILLARY RODHAM CLINTON

AMERICA'S FIRST LADY

Chocolate Chip Cookies

1 1/2 CUPS ALL-PURPOSE FLOUR

1 TEASPOON SALT

1 TEASPOON BAKING SODA

1 CUP SOLID VEGETABLE SHORTENING

1 CUP PACKED LIGHT BROWN SUGAR

1/2 CUP SUGAR

1 TEASPOON VANILLA

2 EGGS

2 CUPS OLD-FASHIONED ROLLED OATS

12-OUNCE PACKAGE (2 CUPS) SEMISWEET CHOCOLATE CHIPS

1. Preheat oven to 350°F. Combine flour, salt, and baking soda.

2. Beat together shortening, sugars, and vanilla in large bowl until creamy. Add eggs one at a time, beating until light and fluffy. Gradually beat in flour mixture and rolled oats. Stir in chocolate chips.

3. Drop batter by well-rounded teaspoons onto baking sheets. Bake 8 to 10 minutes or until golden. Cool cookies on sheets on wire rack for 2 minutes. Transfer cookies to wire rack to cool completely.

Cookies will lose their shape when placed on a hot cookie sheet. Try to cool the pan or rotate your pans. To avoid overbaking cookies, remove them from the oven a few minutes before they are done — the hot pan will continue to bake them.

$\mathcal{B}$ILL COSBY   ACTOR/COMEDIAN

Mouthwatering Bread Pudding

1 PINT HALF AND HALF
1 CUP WHIPPING CREAM
1/2 CUP (1 STICK) BUTTER
1/2 CUP HONEY
2 TEASPOONS VANILLA

PINCH OF NUTMEG
1 EGG, BEATEN
6 TO 7 SLICES STALE BREAD
FRESH GRAPES (YES, THAT'S CORRECT)

1. Combine half and half, cream, butter, and honey in saucepan and heat slowly until warm. Stir in vanilla, nutmeg, and egg.

2. Preheat oven to 450°F. Butter a 13 × 9 × 2-inch glass baking dish. Tear bread into bite-size pieces. Place layer of bread in dish, then layer of grapes, ending with layer of bread on top.

3. Pour milk mixture over bread and grapes, covering all of the bread. If needed, add more milk. Cover dish with foil and place in pan of boiling water. Bake 10 minutes. Reduce heat to 350°F and bake 35 to 40 minutes more. Great hot or cold.

Serves 6 to 8.

Grapes should be plump and firmly attached to a green stem. Grapes do not ripen off the vine, so be certain that they are ripe when selected. When refrigerated, grapes will last 5 to 7 days.

$\mathcal{B}$OB COSTAS SPORTSCASTER

Dolmas

FRESH GRAPE LEAVES OR 1 JAR OR CAN
   GRAPE LEAVES IN BRINE

1 POUND GROUND SIRLOIN

2 EGGS, BEATEN

1 MEDIUM ONION, CHOPPED

1/2 CUP UNCOOKED RICE

1/4 CUP CHOPPED PARSLEY

1 TABLESPOON CHOPPED FRESH MINT
   LEAVES

1/4 CUP ICE WATER

SALT AND PEPPER

32-OUNCE CAN CHICKEN BROTH

For Sauce:

3 EGGS

3 LEMONS

HOT BROTH FROM DOLMAS

1. If using fresh grape leaves, soak in hot water 10 minutes to soften. If using jar or can of grape leaves, rinse in warm water. Remove hard stem ends and place leaves shiny side down.

2. Combine meat, 2 beaten eggs, onion, rice, parsley, mint, ice water, and salt and pepper in large bowl.

3. Place small amount of meat mixture in center of each leaf and roll up, folding in sides to enclose filling.

4. Layer stuffed leaves in saucepan. Place plate over top to hold firmly in place. Pour chicken broth over leaves, cover and simmer about 50 minutes.

5. Make sauce while grape leaves are cooking. Beat 3 eggs, add juice of 3 lemons, slowly beat in hot chicken broth; sauce should be fluffy and foamy. Pour over dolmas.

Serves 6.

Greek and Middle Eastern cooks often use grape leaves to wrap foods for cooking. Fresh grape leaves are usually not available, so unless you have grapevines or own a vineyard, you will have to use canned or bottled leaves packed in brine. They are available at Greek and Middle Eastern groceries and most supermarkets.

$\mathcal{K}$ATIE COURIC TELEVISION PERSONALITY

Lemon Loves

For Crust:

1 CUP (2 STICKS) BUTTER
1/2 CUP CONFECTIONERS' SUGAR

2 CUPS ALL-PURPOSE FLOUR
PINCH OF SALT

1. Preheat oven to 350°F. Blend dry ingredients. Cut in butter until mixture is crumbly.
2. Press crust into lightly greased 13 × 9 × 2-inch pan. Bake 20 minutes while preparing filling.

For Filling:

4 EGGS
2 CUPS SUGAR
6 TABLESPOONS ALL-PURPOSE FLOUR

6 TABLESPOONS FRESH LEMON JUICE
GRATED PEEL OF 1 LEMON
CONFECTIONERS' SUGAR

3. With beater, combine eggs, sugar, flour, lemon juice, and lemon peel. Spread on top of baked crust.
4. Return to oven and bake 25 minutes. When cool, dust with confectioners' sugar and cut into bite-size squares.

Makes 117 squares.

CATHY LEE CROSBY — ACTRESS

Delicious Low-fat Fajitas

2 RIPE TOMATOES
2 RIPE AVOCADOS
4 BONELESS, SKINLESS CHICKEN BREASTS, SLICED INTO STRIPS
CHILI POWDER
GROUND CUMIN
2 GARLIC CLOVES, CHOPPED
SALT

RED PEPPER SAUCE
1 MEDIUM ONION, SLICED
NONFAT 6-INCH FLOUR TORTILLAS
SHREDDED CHEDDAR CHEESE
NONFAT SOUR CREAM
SALSA, FRESH IF POSSIBLE
LIME AND HOT PEPPERS FOR GARNISH

1. Cut tomatoes and avocado into 1/2-inch chunks. Place chicken strips in bowl with chili powder, cumin, garlic, salt, and red pepper sauce. Toss and set aside.

2. Sauté onion until lightly browned and place in small dish. In same skillet, sauté chicken until lightly browned and tender, about 4 minutes. Add cooked onion to chicken in skillet and mix gently to combine.

3. Spoon 1/8 of chicken mixture down center of warmed tortilla. Top with 1/8 of tomato/avocado mixture. Sprinkle with Cheddar cheese; spoon on sour cream and salsa. Fold sides of tortilla to enclose filling. Garnish with lime and hot peppers.

Serves 4.

Avocados are available all year round. They should be fresh in appearance, and the color should range from green to purple-black. They should feel heavy for their size and be slightly firm. Ripen avocados quickly by placing them in a brown paper bag and setting in a warm place. Or place them in a plastic bag with a piece of banana peel. Refrigerate and use within 5 days after ripening. Avocados will not ripen in the refrigerator.

$\mathcal{M}$ARIO CUOMO   FORMER GOVERNOR OF NEW YORK

Spinach Frittata

2 PACKAGES (10 OUNCES EACH) CHOPPED
  FROZEN SPINACH
3 CUPS COTTAGE CHEESE
1 CUP PLAIN BREAD CRUMBS

1/2 CUP GRATED ROMANO CHEESE
5 EGGS
PAPRIKA

1. Preheat oven to 350°F. Boil spinach 30 seconds; drain thoroughly. Blend with cottage cheese, 3/4 cup bread crumbs, and Romano cheese.

2. In separate bowl, beat 3 eggs well and blend in spinach mixture.

3. Lightly oil bottom of 9 × 9-inch baking dish and sprinkle in remaining bread crumbs. Place pan in oven until crumbs are golden brown, 3 to 5 minutes.

4. Spread spinach mixture evenly in baking dish. Beat remaining 2 eggs and pour evenly over spinach. Sprinkle with paprika. Bake 45 minutes. Cool about 10 minutes before cutting.

Serves 9.

From Italy, Romano is a yellow-white cheese with a greenish-black surface and a sharp flavor. It has a hard, granular texture and is available in wedges or grated. It is similar to Parmesan but made with whole milk, giving it a higher fat content.

PHYLLIS DILLER COMEDIENNE/ACTRESS

Seriously Simple Seafood Sublime

3 LARGE UNCOOKED SHRIMP, SHELLED
3 MUSSELS

5 CLAMS
5 OUNCES FILLET OF SOLE

1. Preheat oven to 350°F. Place all ingredients in baking dish. Prepare sauce.

For Sauce:

1 CUP WHITE WINE

1 CUP TOMATO SAUCE

2. Combine wine and sauce and mix well. Pour mixture over seafood. Bake 20 minutes. Serve over rice in flat soup bowls. The juice is divine!

Serves 2 to 3.

When buying fresh fish, check for the following:
- Skin should be firm, elastic, shiny, and not faded. Skin should spring back when finger pressure is exerted.
- Eyes should be bright, clear, and somewhat bulging. The eyes of stale fish are usually cloudy and sunken.
- Scales should be bright, shiny, and tight to skin, not falling off.
- Gills should have no slime, be reddish pink and clean looking, not grayish.
- Fish should never smell "fishy."

ELIZABETH DOLE

FORMER PRESIDENT, AMERICAN RED CROSS

Green Bean Casserole

2 CANS (16 OUNCES EACH) FRENCH-STYLE
  GREEN BEANS, DRAINED (RESERVE LIQUID)
10 1/2-OUNCE CAN CREAM OF MUSHROOM
  SOUP
2.8-OUNCE CAN DURKEE FRENCH-FRIED
  ONIONS
1/2 CUP BEAN LIQUID OR MILK
1/8 TEASPOON PEPPER

1. Preheat oven to 350°F. Drain beans and mix with soup, 1/2 can fried onions, bean liquid, and pepper. Spread in casserole.

2. Bake uncovered 25 minutes. Top with remaining onions and bake 5 minutes longer.

Serves 6.

Quiche Lorraine

8-INCH PIE SHELL
3 EGGS
1 CUP GRATED CHEDDAR CHEESE
1 CUP MILK
1 TABLESPOON CHOPPED ONION
PINCH EACH OF SALT AND PEPPER
1/4 CUP CHOPPED HAM OR BACON

1. Preheat oven to 400°F. Bake pie shell until lightly browned. Let cool.

2. Reduce oven temperature to 350°F. Beat eggs in medium bowl. Add cheese, milk, onion, and salt and pepper.

3. Spread ham or bacon in pie shell; add egg mixture. Bake 20 minutes. Let quiche cool slightly before serving.

Serves 6.

Green peas are good prepared this way, too. Top with grated Cheddar cheese.

*J*OHN ELWAY   CHAMPION QUARTERBACK

Hamburger Soup

2 MEDIUM ONIONS, CHOPPED

1 GARLIC CLOVE, MINCED

2 TABLESPOONS OLIVE OR VEGETABLE OIL
OR BUTTER

3 POUNDS GROUND BEEF

3 CANS (14 1/2 OUNCES EACH) BEEF STOCK

28-OUNCE CAN ROTEL DICED TOMATOES
WITH GREEN CHILES

15-OUNCE CAN TOMATO SAUCE

1 CUP DICED UNPEELED POTATOES

1 CUP DICED PEELED CARROTS

1 CUP DICED CELERY

14 1/2-OUNCE CAN FRENCH-STYLE GREEN
BEANS

1 CUP DRY RED WINE

1 TABLESPOON CHOPPED PARSLEY

1/2 TEASPOON DRIED BASIL

SALT AND PEPPER

1. Sauté onions and garlic in oil in large stockpot until softened. Set aside.
   Brown ground beef. Drain fat and add meat to onions and garlic.

2. Add remaining ingredients to stockpot and simmer until vegetables are
   tender, approximately 1 hour. Season with salt and pepper to taste.
   Serve with warm bread.

Serves 8 to 10.

JANET EVANS   OLYMPIC CHAMPION — SWIMMING

Lasagna — Fast!

1 1/2 POUNDS GROUND BEEF (GROUND TURKEY MAY BE SUBSTITUTED)

16-OUNCE JAR SPAGHETTI SAUCE

1 EGG

1 POUND RICOTTA CHEESE

1 POUND COTTAGE CHEESE

2 TEASPOONS DRIED BASIL

2 TEASPOONS DRIED OREGANO

9 LASAGNA NOODLES

4 CUPS (1 POUND) GRATED MOZZARELLA CHEESE

1/4 CUP WATER

GRATED PARMESAN CHEESE

1. Brown ground beef; drain fat. Stir spaghetti sauce into beef.

2. Preheat oven to 400°F. Mix egg, ricotta, cottage cheese, basil, and oregano in large bowl. Place 3 lasagna noodles on bottom of 13 × 9 × 2-inch pan. Spread 1/3 of meat mixture over noodles. Spread half of cheese mixture over meat. Sprinkle with grated mozzarella. Place 3 noodles on top and repeat above steps. Add remaining 3 lasagna noodles and cover with remaining meat and mozzarella. Pour 1/4 cup water around edges of pan and cover with foil.

3. Bake 1 hour or until noodles are tender. If desired, sprinkle finished lasagna with additional mozzarella and brown under broiler for 5 minutes. Remove from oven and sprinkle with grated Parmesan cheese.

Serves 8.

This is a great dish because it's easy to make and you don't have to boil the noodles beforehand. My mom would always make it and then put it in the fridge. She'd take me to practice, have my dad put it in the oven when he came home from work, and it would be ready as soon as we came home from practice!

LINDA EVANS   ACTRESS

Veal Specialburger

SEASONING SALT
PEPPER
2 POUNDS GROUND WHITE VEAL
1 LARGE FIRM TOMATO, DICED
4 LARGE MUSHROOMS, DICED

10 LARGE STUFFED GREEN OLIVES, DICED
10-OUNCE PACKAGE SHARP CHEDDAR CHEESE, DICED
1/2 LARGE GREEN BELL PEPPER, SEEDED AND DICED

1. Mix a little seasoning salt and pepper into veal. Add diced tomato, mushrooms, olives, cheese, and green pepper. Mix veal mixture with fork, not hands.
2. Form into patties, being careful not to overwork veal. Broil, grill, or sauté to desired doneness.

Serves 8.

Veal has less fat than any meat and usually comes from young milk-fed calves. It is costly but has fewer hormones than beef and is very tender.

DOUGLAS FAIRBANKS, JR. ACTOR

Doug's Favorite Pot Roast

3-POUND BOTTOM ROUND BEEF ROAST

1/4 CUP (1/2 STICK) BUTTER

3 CARROTS

4 CELERY STALKS, CHOPPED

1/2 CUP CHOPPED ONION

1 GARLIC CLOVE, MINCED

1/4 POUND MUSHROOMS, CHOPPED

10 1/2-OUNCE CAN BEEF CONSOMMÉ

1/2 CUP DRY RED WINE

2 TEASPOONS SALT

1/8 TEASPOON PEPPER

1/2 TEASPOON PAPRIKA

1 TABLESPOON CAPERS

1/4 CUP ALL-PURPOSE FLOUR (OPTIONAL)

1 CUP SOUR CREAM

1. Brown roast in butter in large Dutch oven. Add carrots, celery, onion, and garlic and cook until onion is limp. Add mushrooms.

2. Preheat oven to 350°F. Combine half the consommé with wine, salt, pepper, paprika, and capers. Add to beef. Cover and bake 2 hours or until meat is tender.

3. Transfer meat to warm platter. Skim excess fat from juices. With slotted spoon, remove most of vegetables and puree. Return puree to pan. Combine flour, if desired, with remaining consommé and stir into pan with puree. If not using flour, just add consommé. Cook until sauce boils and thickens. Stir in sour cream; do not boil. Serve sauce over meat. I do not use the flour; you'll love this recipe!

Serves 4 to 6.

A Dutch oven is a large pot or kettle, usually made of cast iron, with a tight-fitting lid so steam cannot readily escape. It's used for moist-cooking methods such as braising and stewing. Dutch ovens are available at most retail cookware and hardware stores.

★ ★ ★ ★ ★ ★ ★ ★ ★ ★ ★ ★ ★ ★ ★ ★ ★ ★ ★ ★

Custard Rice Pudding

3/4 CUP INSTANT RICE
1/4 CUP SUGAR
1/4 CUP RAISINS
3 CUPS MILK
1/2 TEASPOON SALT
3 EGGS, BEATEN
1 TEASPOON VANILLA

1. Combine rice, sugar, raisins, milk, and salt in saucepan and bring to rolling boil, stirring often. Cover and simmer 10 minutes.
2. Preheat oven to 375°F. Combine eggs and vanilla in 1 1/2-quart baking dish. Add rice mixture and blend well. Place baking dish in pan filled 1 inch deep with hot water. Bake 25 minutes, stirring after 10 minutes.

Serves 8.

DIANNE FEINSTEIN

UNITED STATES SENATOR—CALIFORNIA

San Francisco Seasoned Shrimp

3 TABLESPOONS OLIVE OIL

2 TABLESPOONS FRESH LEMON JUICE

SALT AND PEPPER

1 POUND SHRIMP, COOKED, SHELLED, AND DEVEINED

1 LARGE ONION

3 TABLESPOONS CHOPPED PIMIENTO

1/4 CUP SLICED BLACK OLIVES

1 LEMON, CUT INTO WEDGES

1. Mix olive oil, lemon juice, and salt and pepper. Add shrimp to marinade. Marinate at least 2 to 3 hours, or in refrigerator overnight.

2. Slice onion into rings and mix into marinated shrimp. Add pimiento and olive slices before serving. Garnish with lemon wedges.

Serves 4.

Strawberry Cheesecake

For Crust:

1 1/4 CUPS GRAHAM CRACKER CRUMBS
5 TABLESPOONS SUGAR
1/4 CUP (1/2 STICK) BUTTER, MELTED

Mix and press into bottom of 9-inch springform pan. Set aside.

For Filling:

3 PACKAGES (8 OUNCES EACH) CREAM CHEESE
3/4 CUP SUGAR
5 TEASPOONS CORNSTARCH
3 EGGS
1 EGG YOLK
2/3 CUP STRAWBERRY LIQUEUR
1 1/4 TEASPOONS VANILLA

1. Preheat oven to 350°F. Mix cream cheese, sugar, and cornstarch. Add eggs one at a time, beating well after each addition. Add egg yolk and beat well. Add liqueur and vanilla and blend well.

2. Pour mixture over crust. Bake 10 minutes. Reduce oven temperature to 200°F and bake 1 hour and 20 minutes or until center is no longer wet or shiny. Run knife around edge of cheesecake. Chill, uncovered, overnight.

For Topping:

2 CUPS SLICED FRESH STRAWBERRIES
1 1/2 CUPS WATER
1/2 CUP SUGAR
1 1/2 TEASPOONS CORNSTARCH

Combine strawberries, water, sugar, and cornstarch in saucepan and bring to boil, stirring gently. Cool. Top cheesecake with strawberry mixture or serve on the side.

Serves 6 to 8.

Never hull strawberries until they have been washed or they will absorb too much water and become mushy. Don't wash or hull until you are ready to eat them. Store strawberries in the refrigerator in a plastic colander, allowing air to circulate around them.

MICHAEL FEINSTEIN SINGER/PIANIST

Salmon Loaf Supreme

15-OUNCE CAN RED SALMON
2 EGGS, BEATEN
GENEROUS 1/2 CUP SOUR CREAM
2 TABLESPOONS FRESH LEMON JUICE
SALT AND PEPPER
2.8-OUNCE CAN FRENCH-FRIED ONION RINGS

1. Preheat oven to 350°F. Drain, skin, and remove bones from salmon. Add eggs, sour cream, and lemon juice and mix well. Season with salt and pepper to taste. Fold in onion rings. Pour into 9 × 5-inch loaf pan.

2. Bake about 40 minutes, or longer if necessary, until lightly browned and puffy.

Serves 4.

Brownie Meringues

2 EGG WHITES
PINCH OF SALT
1/2 TEASPOON VINEGAR
1/2 TEASPOON VANILLA
1/2 CUP SUGAR
6-OUNCE PACKAGE (1 CUP) SEMISWEET CHOCOLATE CHIPS, MELTED AND COOLED
3/4 CUP CHOPPED WALNUTS

1. Preheat oven to 350°F. Beat egg whites with salt, vinegar, and vanilla until soft peaks form. Gradually add sugar, beating to stiff peaks. Fold in chocolate and nuts.

2. Drop meringue by teaspoons onto greased cookie sheets. Bake 10 minutes. Let cool briefly before removing from pan, then cool completely on wire racks.

Makes 3 dozen.

$\mathscr{P}$EGGY FLEMING

Olympic Champion — Figure Skating

Honey Sesame Pork Tenderloin

1/2 CUP SOY SAUCE

2 GARLIC CLOVES, MINCED

1 TABLESPOON GRATED FRESH GINGER
OR 1 TEASPOON GROUND GINGER

1 TABLESPOON SESAME OIL

1 POUND WHOLE PORK TENDERLOIN

1/4 CUP HONEY

2 TABLESPOONS PACKED BROWN SUGAR

1/4 CUP SESAME SEEDS

1. Combine soy sauce, garlic, ginger, and sesame oil. Place tenderloin in heavy plastic bag; pour soy mixture over to coat. Marinate 2 hours at room temperature or overnight in refrigerator.

2. Preheat oven to 375°F. Remove pork from marinade and pat dry. Mix honey and brown sugar in shallow plate. Place sesame seeds on separate shallow plate. Roll pork in honey mixture, coating well; then roll in sesame seeds.

3. Roast tenderloin 20 to 30 minutes, or until meat thermometer inserted into center reaches 160°F. Transfer to serving platter and slice thin to serve.

Serves 4.

Caramelized Lemon Tart

For Tart Shell:

2 1/2 CUPS ALL-PURPOSE FLOUR
PINCH OF SALT (OPTIONAL)
3 TABLESPOONS SUGAR
1 CUP (2 STICKS) COLD UNSALTED BUTTER, CUT INTO PIECES
1/4 CUP ICE WATER
2 LARGE EGG YOLKS, BEATEN

1. Combine flour, salt, and sugar in medium bowl. Cut in butter with pastry blender or fork until mixture resembles coarse meal.

2. Beat together water and egg yolks. Drizzle into flour mixture, stirring with fork; add just enough liquid to make pastry hold together. Shape dough into flat round, wrap in plastic, and chill at least 1 hour or overnight.

3. Preheat oven to 375°F. Roll dough on lightly floured surface to 1/8-inch thickness. Press into bottom and sides of 12-inch tart pan. Run rolling pin across top of tart pan to trim. Carefully line pastry with aluminum foil and weight with beans, rice, or pastry weights.

4. Bake 10 to 15 minutes or until pastry begins to color around edges. Remove weights and foil and continue to bake 10 to 12 minutes, until pastry is browned. Cool completely on wire rack before filling.

Makes one 12-inch tart shell.

For Filling:

2 CUPS SUGAR
1 CUP STRAINED FRESH LEMON JUICE
12 LARGE EGG YOLKS
GRATED PEEL OF 2 LEMONS
1 CUP (2 STICKS) UNSALTED BUTTER, CUT INTO PIECES
12-INCH TART SHELL, BAKED AND COOLED IN PAN WITH REMOVABLE BOTTOM *(see recipe above)*
SUGAR FOR CARAMELIZING TOP OF TART

1. Combine 2 cups sugar and lemon juice in large stainless steel bowl. Strain in yolks. Whisk to combine.

2. Set bowl over pot of simmering water and whisk until mixture thickens, 15 to 20 minutes. Cook an additional 5 minutes.

3. Remove bowl from heat and stir in lemon peel. Stir in butter piece by piece until completely melted. Pour lemon mixture into prepared tart shell. Chill until firm, at least 1 hour.

4. Preheat broiler. Remove outer ring from tart pan and place tart on baking sheet. Place outer ring upside down on tart crust to protect pastry from burning. Sift sugar evenly over top of tart and place under broiler. Watch tart closely to keep from burning. Remove tart when top is evenly browned.

Makes one 12-inch tart.

Submerging a lemon in hot water for 15 minutes before squeezing will yield almost twice the amount of juice. Or try warming lemons in the oven or microwave briefly minutes before squeezing.

$\mathcal{J}$OE FRAZIER CHAMPION BOXER

Smokin' Joe's Chicken

2 POUNDS BONELESS CHICKEN BREASTS
1 SMALL ONION, MINCED
1 GARLIC CLOVE, CRUSHED
2 TABLESPOONS CRUSHED RED PEPPER
2 LEMONS

1 CUP HONEY
1 CUP KETCHUP
1/4 CUP DICED WALNUTS
1 NAVEL ORANGE, SLICED
FRESH PARSLEY SPRIGS

1. Wash chicken thoroughly and place in shallow pan. Preheat oven to 325°F.

2. Toss onion, garlic, and pepper over chicken. Squeeze lemons over chicken.

3. Combine honey and ketchup in saucepan. Simmer 15 minutes. Brush ketchup and honey glaze over chicken. Sprinkle with walnuts. Bake until very little juice is running out of chicken when pricked with fork, about 15 minutes.

4. Place chicken on serving plate and decorate with orange slices and parsley.

Serves 4 to 6.

JAMES GARNER   ACTOR

W. W. Bumgarner's Chili

6 POUNDS GROUND BEEF
3 LARGE ONIONS, FINELY CHOPPED
32-OUNCE CAN TOMATO SAUCE
6 HEAPING TABLESPOONS CHILI POWDER
1 HEAPING TABLESPOON GARLIC POWDER
2 HEAPING TABLESPOONS GROUND CUMIN

2 HEAPING TABLESPOONS DRIED OREGANO
1 TEASPOON CRUSHED JALAPEÑO
2 TO 3 TABLESPOONS ALL-PURPOSE FLOUR
  (OPTIONAL)
SALT AND PEPPER

1. Brown ground beef in large stockpot. Add onions and tomato sauce and simmer until onions are tender.

2. Add chili powder, garlic powder, cumin, oregano, and jalapeño. Add water to cover mixture by 1/4 inch and stir well. Simmer 1 1/2 to 2 hours, stirring often and adding water if needed.

3. Skim off any grease. For thicker chili, combine 2 to 3 tablespoons flour with a little cold water and add to chili. Stir well. Season with salt and pepper to taste.

Serves 12.

This is my dad's own recipe for chili that he always made me. It's my favorite!

MITCH GAYLORD

OLYMPIC CHAMPION — GYMNASTICS

Spicy Tuna Pasta

1 TABLESPOON OLIVE OIL	CRUSHED RED PEPPER
1 GARLIC CLOVE, CHOPPED	BLACK PEPPER
8 RIPE ROMA TOMATOES, DICED	OREGANO
FRESH BASIL	SALT
1/2 CUP V-8 JUICE	GARLIC SALT
1 TABLESPOON DIJON MUSTARD	WHITE WINE
FRESH LEMON JUICE	6-OUNCE CAN TUNA, DRAINED

1. Heat olive oil in large sauté pan and add garlic. Add tomatoes and basil to taste. Simmer, stirring occasionally, 5 minutes.

2. Add V-8 juice and mustard, then season with lemon juice, crushed red pepper, black pepper, oregano, salt, and garlic salt to taste. Cook over medium heat for another couple of minutes and add some white wine as desired.

3. Finally, add tuna and just heat through. Pour sauce over your favorite pasta.

Serves 2 to 4.

PHYLLIS GEORGE

TELEVISION PERSONALITY/COMMENTATOR

Hot Chicken Salad

4 CUPS CUBED COOKED CHICKEN
2 CANS (10 1/4 OUNCES EACH) CREAM OF CHICKEN SOUP
2 CUPS CHOPPED CELERY
2 SMALL ONIONS, CHOPPED
1 CUP SLIVERED ALMONDS
1 CUP MAYONNAISE
2 CANS (5 OUNCES EACH) WATER CHESTNUTS
2 CUPS GRATED CHEDDAR CHEESE
1 TEASPOON SALT
1 TEASPOON PEPPER
POTATO CHIPS FOR TOPPING

1. Preheat oven to 350°F. Combine all ingredients. Pour mixture into 13 × 9 × 2-inch pan. Crumble potato chips on top.

2. Bake about 45 minutes or until hot and bubbly.

Serves 12.

Carrot Soufflé

1 POUND CARROTS, PEELED, COOKED, AND PUREED
3 EGGS, BEATEN
1/3 CUP SUGAR
3 TABLESPOONS ALL-PURPOSE FLOUR
1 TABLESPOON VANILLA
3/4 CUP (1 1/2 STICKS) BUTTER, MELTED
PINCH OF NUTMEG
1 CUP CRUSHED CORNFLAKES
2 TABLESPOONS BROWN SUGAR

1. Preheat oven to 350°F. Butter 8 × 8-inch casserole or 8-inch round soufflé dish. Combine carrots, eggs, sugar, flour, vanilla, 1/2 cup butter, and nutmeg in a medium mixing bowl. Pour into prepared dish.

2. Combine cornflakes, brown sugar, and remaining 1/4 cup butter and sprinkle on top of carrot mixture.

3. Bake 45 minutes or until topping is browned.

Serves 6.

Carrots should have smooth skins and good orange color and be well formed. Do not purchase if wilted or cracked, or if tops are green. Keep refrigerated. The tops should be removed before storage; they will drain the carrots of moisture, making them limp and dry.

Coca-Cola Cake

2 CUPS ALL-PURPOSE FLOUR

2 CUPS SUGAR

1 CUP (2 STICKS) BUTTER

1 TABLESPOON COCOA POWDER

1 CUP COCA-COLA

1/2 CUP BUTTERMILK

1 TEASPOON BAKING SODA

2 EGGS, BEATEN

1 TEASPOON VANILLA

1 1/2 CUPS MINIATURE MARSHMALLOWS

1. Preheat oven to 350°F. Grease 13 × 9 × 2-inch pan. Combine flour and sugar.

2. Bring butter, cocoa, and Coca-Cola to boil in saucepan. Pour over sugar and flour mixture and mix well. Add buttermilk, baking soda, eggs, vanilla, and marshmallows and beat well. Pour into pan. Bake 30 to 40 minutes, or until knife inserted in center comes out clean. Prepare topping.

For Topping:

1/2 CUP (1 STICK) BUTTER

2 TABLESPOONS COCA-COLA

1 TABLESPOON COCOA POWDER

1 POUND (4 CUPS) CONFECTIONERS' SUGAR

3. Mix butter, Coca-Cola, and cocoa in saucepan and bring to boil. Pour over powdered sugar in large bowl and beat well.

4. Ice cake while the topping is hot.

Serves 12.

When making frosting, try adding a pinch of baking soda to the powdered sugar. The baking soda helps retain liquid so the frosting won't crumble and dry as quickly.

£EEZA GIBBONS   TELEVISION HOST/ENTERTAINER

Rustic Apple Tart

For Pastry:

1 1/4 CUPS ALL-PURPOSE FLOUR
3/4 TEASPOON GRATED LEMON PEEL
1/2 TEASPOON SALT
1/2 CUP (1 STICK) CHILLED UNSALTED
   BUTTER, CUT INTO SMALL PIECES

3 1/2 TABLESPOONS VERY COLD WATER
1 1/2 TEASPOONS FRESH LEMON JUICE

1. Blend flour, lemon peel, and salt in food processor with metal blade. Cut in butter using on/off turns until mixture resembles coarse meal.

2. Combine cold water and lemon juice. With machine running, pour through feed tube and process just until dough begins to gather; do not overprocess.

3. Gather dough into ball and flatten into disk. Wrap dough in plastic and refrigerate at least 30 minutes. Prepare filling.

For Filling:

2 GOLDEN DELICIOUS APPLES, PEELED
   AND CORED
1 GRANNY SMITH APPLE, PEELED AND
   CORED
2 TEASPOONS FRESH LEMON JUICE
2 TEASPOONS BRANDY

1/4 CUP SUGAR
1/2 TEASPOON NUTMEG
1/4 TEASPOON CINNAMON
3 TABLESPOONS UNSALTED BUTTER
CONFECTIONERS' SUGAR

4. Place rack in center of oven and preheat to 425°F. Cut apples into 1/4-inch-thick slices. Toss with lemon juice and brandy in large bowl. Combine 1/4 cup sugar, nutmeg, and cinnamon in small bowl.

5. Roll dough out on lightly floured surface to 12-inch round (do not trim edges). Transfer dough to large cookie sheet.

6. Place sliced apples on pastry, mounding slightly in center and leaving 2-inch border of pastry all around. Sprinkle apples with sugar mixture. Dot with butter. Fold pastry border in over apple filling.

7. Bake tart 15 minutes. Reduce heat to 375°F and bake until pastry is golden brown and filling bubbles, about 35 minutes.

8. Using two spatulas, carefully transfer tart to rack. Cool slightly. Dust tart with confectioners' sugar. Serve warm or at room temperature.

Serves 4 to 6.

Tart dough will turn out better if all ingredients are cold and the dough is not overworked. The dough should also be refrigerated before it is used.

KATHIE LEE GIFFORD

TELEVISION HOST/ENTERTAINER

Mom's Baked Chicken Salad

4 CUPS DICED COOKED CHICKEN
10 1/2-OUNCE CAN CREAM OF CHICKEN SOUP
3/4 CUP MAYONNAISE
2 CUPS DICED CELERY
1/4 CUP WATER CHESTNUTS, DRAINED AND
   SLICED
1 TEASPOON SALT
1 TEASPOON FRESH LEMON JUICE
2/3 CUP GRATED SHARP CHEDDAR CHEESE
1/3 CUP SLICED ALMONDS
1 CUP CRUSHED POTATO CHIPS

1. Mix first seven ingredients and
   spread in 13 × 9 × 2-inch baking
   dish.

2. Preheat oven to 400°F. Mix cheese,
   almonds, and chips and sprinkle on
   top of chicken mixture.

3. Bake 30 minutes.

   Serves 6 to 8.

Banana Nut Bread

2 LARGE OR 3 SMALL BANANAS, PEELED
   AND BROKEN UP
2 EGGS
1 CUP SUGAR
1/4 CUP (1/2 STICK) BUTTER, MELTED
3 TABLESPOONS MILK
2 CUPS ALL-PURPOSE FLOUR
1/2 TEASPOON SALT
1/2 TEASPOON BAKING POWDER
1/2 TEASPOON BAKING SODA
3/4 CUP CHOPPED WALNUTS

1. Preheat oven to 325°F. Spray
   9 × 5-inch loaf pan with nonstick
   vegetable spray.

2. Puree bananas in mixing bowl with
   electric beater. Beat in eggs, sugar,
   butter, and milk.

3. Sift in flour, salt, baking powder,
   and baking soda and stir with
   wooden spoon just to blend. Fold
   in nuts.

4. Spread batter in prepared pan and
   bake until knife inserted in center
   comes out clean, about 1 hour.
   Cool bread in pan.

*Refresh stale potato chips,
crackers, or other crisp
snacks by microwaving for
30 to 45 seconds. Let stand
1 minute to crisp. Cereals
can also be crisped this way.*

$\mathcal{V}$INCE GILL SINGER/SONGWRITER

Peanut Butter Fudge

4 CUPS SUGAR

2 CANS (5 OUNCES EACH) EVAPORATED
MILK (1 1/3 CUPS)

1 CUP (2 STICKS) BUTTER

10-OUNCE PACKAGE PEANUT BUTTER
CHIPS (1 3/4 CUPS)

7-OUNCE JAR MARSHMALLOW CREME

1 CUP FINELY CHOPPED PEANUTS

1 TEASPOON VANILLA

1. Line 8 × 8 × 2-inch baking pan with foil, extending foil over edges. Butter
    foil; set pan aside.

2. Butter sides of heavy 3-quart saucepan. Combine sugar, milk, and butter in
    prepared saucepan and bring to boil, stirring, over medium-high heat.

3. Clip candy thermometer to side of pan. Cook and stir over medium heat to
    236°F soft-ball stage (about 12 minutes).

4. Remove saucepan from heat; remove thermometer. Add peanut butter chips,
    marshmallow creme, peanuts, and vanilla; stir until chips are melted. Spread
    in prepared pan. Score into squares while warm.

5. When firm, cut fudge into squares. Store in refrigerator.

Makes about 3 1/3 pounds or 36 servings.

*A candy thermometer is
used for testing the
temperature of candies,
jams, jellies, syrups, and in
deep fat frying. Choose a
thermometer that registers
from 100°F to 400°F and
that is easy to handle in hot
mixtures. Many come with
adjustable clips to attach
the thermometer to a pan.*

MICKEY GILLEY   SINGER/SONGWRITER

Black Bean and Cheese Nachos

3 1/2 TABLESPOONS REFRIED BLACK BEANS

2 1/2 TABLESPOONS GRATED MONTEREY
 JACK CHEESE

1/4 TEASPOON MINCED JALAPEÑOS

CHILI POWDER

1/2 TEASPOON VEGETABLE OIL

2 1/2 TEASPOONS MINCED GREEN BELL
 PEPPER

1 1/2 TABLESPOONS MINCED GREEN ONION

MINCED GARLIC

WHITE CORN TORTILLA CHIPS

Toppings:

2 TABLESPOONS GRATED MONTEREY
 JACK CHEESE

1 TABLESPOON MINCED RED BELL PEPPER

1 TABLESPOON MINCED GREEN ONION TOPS

1. Combine first four ingredients in heavy pot and cook over low heat until cheese is melted and beans are hot. Cover and keep warm.

2. Sauté pepper, green onion, and garlic over medium-high heat until pepper is tender. Add to bean mixture and stir well.

3. Preheat oven to 375°F. Portion 1 tablespoon bean mixture on each tortilla chip. Top each portion with cheese, pepper, and green onion. Bake until cheese is melted. Serve with salsa and cilantro.

Serves 2.

Vegetarian Tortilla Soup

3 TABLESPOONS OLIVE OIL
2/3 CUP MINCED ONION
1 TEASPOON MINCED GARLIC
1 TEASPOON GROUND CUMIN
1 TEASPOON CHILI POWDER
2/3 CUP PICANTE SAUCE
2 CUPS ENCHILADA SAUCE
2/3 CUP CHOPPED GREEN CHILIES
2 TABLESPOONS CHOPPED JALAPEÑOS
1 CUP VEGETABLE STOCK
1 1/2 TABLESPOONS WORCESTERSHIRE
SAUCE
1 TEASPOON SALT
1/2 TEASPOON PEPPER
2/3 CUP CORN TORTILLAS, CUT INTO THIN
STRIPS
1/3 CUP GRATED CHEDDAR CHEESE

1. Combine all ingredients except
   tortilla strips and Cheddar cheese
   in large pot or kettle and bring
   to boil over high heat. Reduce
   heat and simmer covered for
   about 1 hour.

2. Uncover, add tortilla strips and
   simmer 10 minutes. Ladle soup
   into bowls and sprinkle with
   Cheddar cheese.

   Serves 8.

Southwestern Chicken Salad

10 TOSTADA SHELLS
2 1/2 POUNDS CHICKEN, COOKED AND
CHOPPED
2 1/2 CUPS CHOPPED CELERY
1/2 POUND BACON, FRIED CRISP AND
CRUMBLED
1 CAN CHOPPED GREEN CHILIES
1/2 CUP CHOPPED PEANUTS
1 1/4 CUPS MAYONNAISE
5 CUPS SHREDDED LETTUCE

1. Heat tostada shells in 350°F oven
   5 to 7 minutes to crisp. Let cool.

2. Combine chicken, celery, bacon,
   green chilies, peanuts, and
   mayonnaise. Chill.

3. When ready to serve, fill tostada
   shells with about 1/2 cup lettuce.
   Spoon chicken salad over lettuce.

   Serves 10.

Charcoal-grilled Summer Vegetables

4 SMALL POTATOES
2 SMALL EGGPLANTS
2 ZUCCHINI
2 SUMMER SQUASH
4 RED BELL PEPPERS
1/4 CUP (1/2 STICK) BUTTER, SOFTENED
1 TABLESPOON FRESH OR DRIED BASIL
1 TABLESPOON FRESH OR 1 TEASPOON DRIED THYME
1 GARLIC CLOVE, FINELY CHOPPED
SALT
1/3 CUP GRATED PARMESAN CHEESE

1. Cut all vegetables in half lengthwise. Core pepper and scrape out seeds.

2. Combine butter with the herbs and garlic, and salt to taste. Spread butter over vegetables.

3. Arrange vegetables on grill over medium-high coals, placing potatoes in center where heat is strongest. Cook 10 minutes. Turn and sprinkle with Parmesan cheese. Grill 10 minutes more or until all vegetables are tender.

Serves 6 to 8.

Baked Barbecue Beans

4 CANS (28 OUNCES EACH) PREPARED BAKED BEANS
1 MEDIUM ONION, DICED
1/4 POUND BACON, DICED
1/2 CUP PACKED BROWN SUGAR
1 CUP KETCHUP
1 TABLESPOON MINCED GARLIC
2 CUPS BARBECUE SAUCE
SALT AND PEPPER

1. Preheat oven to 350°F.

2. Sauté onion and bacon until onion is translucent and bacon is cooked. Add to remaining ingredients in casserole. Bake 45 minutes.

Makes 28 servings (4 ounces each).

Mexican Pizza

10 FLOUR TORTILLAS
3 CUPS VEGETABLE OIL FOR FRYING
2 POUNDS GROUND BEEF (PORK, CHICKEN,
    OR TURKEY MAY BE SUBSTITUTED)
1 ENVELOPE TACO SEASONING MIX
1 CUP WATER
4 CUPS (1 POUND) GRATED MONTEREY
    JACK CHEESE
4-OUNCE CAN DICED GREEN CHILIES
14 1/2-OUNCE CAN DICED TOMATOES,
    DRAINED
2 CUPS SLICED BLACK OLIVES

1. Fry tortillas in hot oil until crisp;
   drain on paper towels and set
   aside.

2. Brown beef in large skillet; drain.
   Add taco seasoning mix and water
   and bring to boil. Reduce heat and
   simmer uncovered 25 minutes,
   stirring occasionally.

3. Preheat oven to 425°F. Layer
   ingredients in following order
   on each fried tortilla: seasoned
   meat, grated cheese, diced chilies,
   diced tomatoes, and sliced olives.
   Bake 5 minutes.

   Serves 10.

Western Chili

3 CUPS DRIED RED BEANS
6 CUPS WATER
2 TO 3 BAY LEAVES
2 POUNDS GROUND BEEF
1/2 POUND PORK SAUSAGE MEAT
3 CUPS CHOPPED ONION
1 TABLESPOON MINCED GARLIC
1 TABLESPOON CHILI POWDER
3 CANS (8 OUNCES EACH) TOMATO SAUCE
1 TEASPOON RED PEPPER FLAKES
1 TEASPOON CURRY POWDER
1 TABLESPOON GROUND CUMIN
1 TABLESPOON SALT
1/4 TEASPOON HOT PEPPER SAUCE
1/8 TEASPOON CINNAMON

1. Soak beans overnight. The next
   day, drain beans and place in large
   pot with 6 cups water and bay
   leaves. Simmer until tender, about
   45 minutes. Drain and remove
   bay leaves.

2. Brown ground beef and sausage
   meat with onion and garlic about
   10 minutes; drain. Add to beans
   with chili powder, tomato sauce,
   red pepper flakes, curry powder,
   cumin, salt, hot pepper sauce, and
   cinnamon. Simmer 1 hour.

   Serves 8 to 10.

*To reduce gassiness caused
by beans, try "Beano." It
can neutralize the sugar in
the beans that causes gas
production in the body. You
can also tackle the problem
by adding a teaspoon of
fennel seed to the beans'
soaking water.*

Strawberry Shortcake

For Strawberries:

3 PINTS FRESH STRAWBERRIES, WASHED,
   STEMMED, AND SLICED
1/4 CUP SUGAR OR HONEY
2 TEASPOONS ORANGE JUICE

Combine berries, sweetener, and orange juice. Let stand at room temperature
1 hour.

For Shortcakes:

2 CUPS SIFTED ALL-PURPOSE FLOUR
1/4 CUP SUGAR
4 TEASPOONS BAKING POWDER
1/2 TEASPOON SALT
GRATED PEEL OF 1 ORANGE

1/4 CUP (1/2 STICK) BUTTER OR MARGARINE
1/4 CUP SOLID VEGETABLE SHORTENING
1/2 CUP SOUR CREAM
2 CUPS WHIPPING CREAM

1. Sift together dry ingredients. Add orange peel. Work in butter and shortening
   with a fork, then lightly mix in sour cream to form soft dough.
2. On lightly floured board, roll dough about 3/4 inch thick; cut into circles
   about 4 inches wide. Place on ungreased cookie sheet and bake until golden,
   about 12 to 15 minutes.
3. Whip cream. Split shortcakes and fill with half of strawberries and cream.
   Top with remaining strawberries and cream.

   Serves 4.

*J*OHN GLENN

ASTRONAUT/FORMER UNITED STATES SENATOR

Muskingum Chocolate Dew Cake

2 CUPS CAKE FLOUR	1/2 TEASPOON SALT
1 CUP SUGAR	1 CUP COLD WATER
1/4 CUP COCOA POWDER	1 CUP MAYONNAISE
2 TEASPOONS BAKING SODA	1 TEASPOON VANILLA

1. Sift together dry ingredients several times.
2. Mix water, mayonnaise, and vanilla in bowl.
3. Preheat oven to 350°F. Spray two 8-inch round pans with nonstick vegetable spray. Stir mayonnaise mixture into dry ingredients.
4. Divide batter between prepared pans. Bake for 30 minutes or until toothpick inserted in middle comes out clean.
5. Let cool in pans on racks for 10 minutes, turn cakes out on racks, and cool completely. Frost with your favorite chocolate frosting.

Serves 6.

For Chocolate Frosting:

1/3 CUP SOFT BUTTER
3 CUPS SIFTED CONFECTIONERS' SUGAR
3 TABLESPOONS LIGHT CREAM
1 1/2 TEASPOONS VANILLA
3 SQUARES (3 OUNCES EACH) UNSWEETENED
  CHOCOLATE, MELTED

1. Blend butter, confectioners' sugar, and light cream.
2. Add vanilla and melted chocolate and stir until smooth.

Covers 2 layers of 8 or 9 inches.

Tipper Gore   WIFE OF THE VICE PRESIDENT

Spiced Roast Chicken with Mushroom Stuffing

2 TABLESPOONS OLIVE OIL

1 ONION, FINELY CHOPPED

1 TEASPOON GARAM MASALA

4 OUNCES BUTTON OR BROWN MUSHROOMS, CHOPPED

1 CUP COARSELY GRATED PARSNIPS

1 CUP COARSELY GRATED CARROTS

1/4 CUP MINCED WALNUTS

2 TEASPOONS CHOPPED FRESH THYME

1 CUP FRESH WHITE BREAD CRUMBS

1 EGG, BEATEN

SALT AND PEPPER

1 FRESH CHICKEN, ABOUT 3 1/2 POUNDS

1 TABLESPOON MARGARINE

2/3 CUP MARSALA WINE

THYME AND WATERCRESS SPRIGS

SEASONAL VEGETABLES

1. Heat olive oil in large saucepan. Add onion and sauté 2 minutes or until softened. Stir in garam masala and cook 1 minute. Add mushrooms, parsnips, and carrots; cook, stirring, 5 minutes. Remove from heat and stir in walnuts, thyme, bread crumbs, egg, and salt and pepper.

2. Preheat oven to 375°F. Stuff chicken with mushroom mixture; truss. Place breast down in roasting pan; add 1/4 cup water to pan. Roast 45 minutes. Turn chicken breast up and dot with margarine. Roast about 45 more minutes or until meat thermometer inserted in thickest part of thigh (not touching bone) registers 185°F. Transfer to platter and keep warm.

3. Pour off fat from roasting pan. Add Marsala to remaining cooking juices, stirring to scrape up browned bits. Boil over high heat 1 minute to reduce slightly; adjust seasoning.

4. Carve chicken. Garnish with thyme and watercress sprigs. Serve with stuffing, flavored meat juices, and seasonal vegetables.

Serves 4.

Garam masala is an intensely aromatic mixture of ground spices used in making some Indian dishes (the name means "hot spice mixture"). It's available ready mixed at Indian foodstores, or you can grind and mix your own at home.

2 tablespoons coriander seeds; 3-inch cinnamon stick, broken into small pieces; 1 tablespoon cumin seeds; 1 teaspoon whole cloves; 1 teaspoon cardamom pods; 1 tablespoon mace; 1 tablespoon black pepper

Mix all ingredients and grind or pound to fine powder, using electric spice grinder or mortar and pestle. Place in jar; cap tightly, and store in cool, dark place. Makes 5 tablespoons.

TOMMY HILFIGER   FASHION DESIGNER

The Lasagna Recipe

1 POUND GROUND BEEF

1 MEDIUM ONION, CHOPPED

1 GARLIC CLOVE, FINELY CHOPPED

2 TABLESPOONS CHOPPED FRESH PARSLEY

1 TABLESPOON SUGAR

1 TABLESPOON CHOPPED FRESH BASIL
LEAVES

15-OUNCE CAN TOMATO SAUCE

16-OUNCE CAN WHOLE TOMATOES,
UNDRAINED

12 FRESH UNCOOKED LASAGNA NOODLES

1 POUND RICOTTA CHEESE

1/4 CUP GRATED PARMESAN CHEESE

1 TABLESPOON CHOPPED FRESH PARSLEY

1 TABLESPOON CHOPPED FRESH OREGANO
LEAVES

2 CUPS SLICED MOZZARELLA CHEESE

SEA SALT

1. Cook beef, onion, and garlic until meat is browned. Drain. Stir in 2 tablespoons parsley, sugar, basil, and tomato sauce; break up whole tomatoes and add. Simmer 45 minutes.

2. Preheat oven to 350°F. Boil noodles until al dente; drain. Mix ricotta cheese, 1/4 cup Parmesan cheese, 1 tablespoon parsley, and oregano.

3. Spread 1 cup sauce mixture in baking dish. Top with 4 noodles. Spread 1 cup cheese mixture over noodles. Spread with 1 cup sauce mixture. Cover with mozzarella slices. Repeat process until all ingredients are used. Cover with wax paper, then a sheet of foil and bake 30 minutes.

4. Uncover and bake 15 more minutes or until bubbly. Serve with green salad and garlic bread.

Serves 8.

Ricotta is an Italian whey cheese that is most familiar in its fresh, unripened form, when it is white and creamy with a soft, smooth texture and a bland, slightly sweet flavor. It's also available dried, salted, and aged, as a harder grating cheese. Ricotta is an exceptionally versatile cheese, eaten fresh as dessert with fruit or liqueur, and also featured extensively in Italian cooking—especially as a filling for pasta dishes and pastries. It should be used within 24 to 36 hours of opening.

ℳNJELICA HUSTON   ACTRESS

Flourless Chocolate Cake with Chocolate Glaze

For Cake:

12 OUNCES BITTERSWEET (NOT
     UNSWEETENED) OR SEMISWEET
     CHOCOLATE, CHOPPED
3/4 CUP (1 1/2 STICKS) UNSALTED BUTTER,
     CUT INTO PIECES

6 LARGE EGGS, SEPARATED
12 TABLESPOONS SUGAR
2 TEASPOONS VANILLA

1. Preheat oven to 350°F. Butter 9-inch springform pan. Line bottom with parchment paper or waxed paper; butter paper. Wrap outside of pan with foil.

2. In heavy saucepan, stir chocolate and butter over low heat until melted and smooth. Remove from heat. Let cool to lukewarm, stirring often.

3. Using electric mixer, beat egg yolks and 6 tablespoons sugar in large bowl until thick and pale, about 3 minutes. Fold lukewarm chocolate mixture into egg yolk mixture, then fold in vanilla. Using clean, dry beaters, beat egg whites in another large bowl until soft peaks form. Gradually add remaining 6 tablespoons sugar, beating until medium-firm peaks form. Slowly fold egg whites into chocolate mixture. Pour batter into prepared pan.

4. Bake cake until top is puffed and cracked, about 50 minutes. Tester inserted into center should come out with some moist crumbs attached. Cool cake in pan on rack. Cake will fall.

5. Gently press down crusty top to make evenly thick cake. Using small knife, cut around pan sides to loosen cake. Remove pan sides. Place 9-inch-diameter tart pan bottom or cardboard round atop cake and invert cake onto it. Peel off parchment or waxed paper.

For Chocolate Glaze:

1/2 CUP WHIPPING CREAM

1/2 CUP DARK CORN SYRUP

9 OUNCES BITTERSWEET (NOT UNSWEETENED)
 OR SEMISWEET CHOCOLATE, FINELY
 CHOPPED

1. Bring cream and corn syrup to simmer in medium saucepan. Remove from heat. Add chocolate and whisk until melted and smooth.

2. Place cake on rack set over baking sheet. Spread 1/2 cup glaze smoothly over top and sides of cake. Freeze until almost set, about 3 minutes. Pour remaining glaze over cake; smooth top and sides. Chill until glaze is firm, about 1 hour. Serve at room temperature.

Serves 10.

*B*RUCE JENNER OLYMPIC CHAMPION—DECATHLON

All-American Blueberry Muffins

3/4 CUP SOLID VEGETABLE SHORTENING
1 1/2 CUPS SUGAR
3 CUPS ALL-PURPOSE FLOUR
3/4 TEASPOON SALT
4 TEASPOONS BAKING POWDER
1/2 TEASPOON CINNAMON

1/2 TEASPOON NUTMEG
1 1/2 CUPS MILK
3 EGGS
1 TEASPOON VANILLA
1 QUART FRESH BLUEBERRIES

1. Preheat oven to 375°F. Grease 24 muffin cups or line with paper liners. Cream shortening and sugar. In separate bowl, mix all dry ingredients. In another bowl blend milk, eggs, and vanilla.

2. Add dry ingredients and egg mixture alternately to shortening and sugar mixture, blending after each addition. Gently fold in blueberries.

3. Fill muffin cups half full. Bake 25 minutes or until golden.

Makes 24 muffins.

Muffins will slide right out of tins if the hot pan is first placed on a wet towel.

*B*ILLY JOEL SINGER/SONGWRITER

Grilled Tuna and Marinated Cucumber Salad

For Marinade:

2/3 CUP OLIVE OIL

1/4 CUP TERIYAKI SAUCE

JUICE OF 1 LEMON

1 TABLESPOON CHOPPED PARSLEY

SALT AND PEPPER

2 (8 OUNCES EACH) FRESH TUNA STEAKS

1. Combine olive oil, teriyaki sauce, lemon juice, and parsley in glass or ceramic container and mix well. Season with salt and pepper to taste.
2. Place tuna steaks in marinade, making sure fish is completely covered by marinade. Cover and refrigerate overnight.

For Cucumber Salad:

2 CUCUMBERS, WASHED, PEELED, AND
    THINLY SLICED

1/4 CUP WHITE WINE VINEGAR

DASH OF OLIVE OIL

1 TABLESPOON CHOPPED CILANTRO

SALT AND PEPPER

THINLY SLICED ONION (OPTIONAL)

Combine all ingredients in bowl, seasoning to taste with salt and pepper. Cover and refrigerate overnight.

When Ready to Grill:

1. Grill tuna steaks over barbecue, making sure not to overcook. Tuna should be pink inside.
2. Drain cucumber salad. Break tuna into chunks and add to salad.

Serves 2.

This is one of my favorite recipes and should be started a day ahead of time.

LADY BIRD JOHNSON   FORMER FIRST LADY

Cheese Wafers

1 CUP (2 STICKS) BUTTER OR MARGARINE, SOFTENED
2 CUPS ALL-PURPOSE FLOUR
8 OUNCES CHEDDAR CHEESE, GRATED
1 TEASPOON CAYENNE PEPPER
1/2 TEASPOON SALT
2 CUPS RICE KRISPIES CEREAL

1. Preheat oven to 350°F. Cut butter into flour until mixture resembles coarse crumbs. Add cheese and seasonings. Stir in cereal. Drop by small rounds on ungreased cookie sheet and flatten with spoon.

2. Bake about 15 minutes or until lightly browned. Cool on racks.

Makes 5 dozen.

Cheese wafers are a ranch staple, served on all occasions: with salads, with cocktails, or when one of the grandchildren gets the munchies!

Lace Cookies

1/2 CUP ALL-PURPOSE FLOUR
1/2 CUP SHREDDED COCONUT
1/4 CUP LIGHT OR DARK CORN SYRUP
1/4 CUP PACKED BROWN SUGAR
1/2 CUP (1 STICK) MARGARINE
1/2 TEASPOON VANILLA

1. Mix flour and coconut in bowl; set aside. Blend syrup, brown sugar, and margarine in saucepan. Cook over medium heat, stirring constantly, until mixture is bubbly. Remove from heat and stir in vanilla. Gradually blend in flour and coconut mixture.

2. Preheat oven to 325°F. Drop dough by teaspoons 3 to 4 inches apart on ungreased cookie sheet. Bake until lightly browned around edges, about 15 to 20 minutes.

3. Allow cookies to cool about 1 minute before transferring to rack.

Makes 2 dozen.

Lace cookies are served alone or with fresh peach ice cream at the ranch. They're also perfect for that special tea or brunch.

★ ★

EDWARD KENNEDY

UNITED STATES SENATOR, MASSACHUSETTS

Cape Cod Fish Chowder

2 POUNDS FRESH HADDOCK
2 OUNCES SALT PORK, DICED
2 MEDIUM ONIONS, SLICED
1 CUP CHOPPED CELERY
4 LARGE POTATOES, DICED

1 BAY LEAF
4 CUPS MILK
2 TABLESPOONS BUTTER OR MARGARINE
1 TABLESPOON SALT
FRESHLY GROUND PEPPER

1. Simmer haddock in 2 cups water 15 minutes. Drain, and reserve broth. Remove skin and bones from fish.

2. Sauté salt pork in large pot until crisp. Remove salt pork. Sauté onions in pork fat until golden brown. Add fish, celery, potatoes, and bay leaf. Measure reserved fish broth; add boiling water to make 3 cups. Add to pot and simmer 40 minutes. Add milk and butter and heat through. Season with salt and pepper.

Serves 8.

Haddock is a saltwater fish closely related to cod. Low in fat, it has a firm texture and mild flavor. Fresh haddock is available whole or in fillets or steaks, frozen haddock in fillets and steaks. The fish is wonderful baked, grilled, poached, or sautéed.

$\mathscr{A}$LAN KING COMEDIAN

U.S. Open Chili

1/4 CUP OLIVE OIL	1 TABLESPOON GROUND CUMIN
2 CUPS CHOPPED ONION	1 TABLESPOON PEPPER
2 TABLESPOONS MINCED GARLIC	1 TABLESPOON RED PEPPER FLAKES
3/4 CUP DICED GREEN BELL PEPPER	2 TABLESPOONS CHILI POWDER
3/4 CUP DICED RED BELL PEPPER	JUICE OF 1/2 LEMON
SALT AND PEPPER	3 TABLESPOONS DRIED OREGANO
1/4 CUP VEGETABLE OIL	3 TABLESPOONS DRIED THYME
5 POUNDS LEAN GROUND CHUCK	4 BAY LEAVES
2 POUNDS HOT ITALIAN SAUSAGE, CASINGS REMOVED	1 OR 2 SMALL PORK BONES
4 POUNDS FLANK OR SKIRT STEAK, CUBED	1 CUP BEEF BOUILLON
3 CANS (28 OUNCES EACH) ITALIAN PLUM TOMATOES	1 1/2 POUNDS DRIED RED KIDNEY BEANS OR 3 CANS (16 OUNCES EACH) RED KIDNEY BEANS
12-OUNCE CAN TOMATO PASTE	

1. Heat olive oil in heavy 12-inch skillet. Sauté onions, garlic, and bell peppers over medium heat until vegetables are wilted but not brown. Season with salt and pepper and place in heavy 8- or 9-quart pot or Dutch oven.

2. Heat vegetable oil in same skillet. Divide beef into 2 batches. Brown each batch in skillet, breaking up clumps as meat cooks. Sprinkle with salt and pepper and add to pot.

3. Add sausage meat to skillet and brown lightly, breaking up clumps. Add sausage to pot.

4. In same skillet, lightly brown flank or skirt steak in 2 batches, adding oil to skillet if needed. Set cubed beef aside in bowl.

Cut from the beef flank, skirt steak is a long, flat piece of meat that is flavorful but rather tough. If properly cooked, it can be tender and delicious. It's wonderful when marinated. Try it grilled, stuffed, or rolled.

5. Add plum tomatoes with liquid to pot and bring to simmer as you stir in tomato paste, cumin, pepper, red pepper flakes, chili powder, and lemon juice. Add oregano and thyme, rubbing them between your palms. Add bay leaves and pork bones and stir to blend.

6. If you use dried kidney beans, add them now. (If you prefer canned, they will be added later.) Stir in beef bouillon and bring mixture to boil. Reduce heat and simmer, covered, about 3 hours or until mixture begins to thicken and meat is soft. Add cubed beef and continue cooking 3 more hours, stirring frequently and adding bouillon or water if chili seems in danger of scorching. If you use canned kidney beans, drain and rinse under cold running water. Add to chili for last hour of cooking.

7. Store chili in refrigerator up to 5 days. To reheat, bring to boil, reduce heat, and simmer 1 hour, adding bouillon or seasonings as needed. Serve with raw chopped onion and additional red pepper flakes.

Serves about 20.

STEPHEN KING **AUTHOR**

Basic White Bread

2 ENVELOPES DRY YEAST
3 TABLESPOONS SUGAR
3/4 CUP WARM WATER
2 CUPS LUKEWARM MILK
1 TABLESPOON SALT
3 TABLESPOONS SOLID VEGETABLE SHORTENING
8 CUPS ALL-PURPOSE OR BREAD FLOUR
MELTED BUTTER

1. Dissolve yeast and sugar in water. Add milk, salt, shortening, and 1/2 of flour; mix until smooth. Mix in remaining flour until dough is easy to handle.

2. Knead dough on floured surface until smooth — 10 minutes should do it. Place in greased bowl, cover with towel, and let rise until doubled, about 1 hour.

3. Divide dough in half and shape each into loaf. Place in greased 9 × 5-inch loaf pans and brush with melted butter. Let rise another hour.

4. Preheat oven to 425°F. Bake loaves 25 to 30 minutes or until brown. To test doneness, tap to see if loaves sound hollow. Brush again with butter if you like.

Makes 2 loaves.

Baking bread is one of the ways I relax. I like kneading it and I love the smell of it, the way it fills the house and makes your mouth water.

Lunchtime Gloop

1 POUND GROUND BEEF

2 CANS FRANCO-AMERICAN SPAGHETTI (WITHOUT MEATBALLS)

1. Brown beef in large skillet. Add canned spaghetti and cook until heated through.

2. Do not drain hamburger or it won't be properly greasy. Burning this dish will only improve the flavor! Serve with buttered bread.

Serves 6.

My kids love this. I only make it when my wife, Tabby, isn't home. She won't eat it—in fact, doesn't even like to look at it.

ROBIN LEACH   TELEVISION PRODUCER/ENTERTAINER

Rich-and-Famous Chicken

1/2 CUP (1 STICK) UNSALTED BUTTER

3 TABLESPOONS ALL-PURPOSE FLOUR

2 CUPS ESSENCE OF SILVER AND GOLD
(see following recipe)

SALT AND PEPPER

2 LARGE ONIONS, SLICED

1 WHOLE CHICKEN (3 1/2 TO 5 POUNDS),
CUT INTO 8 PIECES

1 CUP CHAMPAGNE

1/4 CUP FRESH BASIL LEAVES, FINELY
CHOPPED (OR 2 TABLESPOONS DRIED)

2 TABLESPOONS FRESH OREGANO, FINELY
CHOPPED (OR 1 TABLESPOON DRIED)

1/2 TEASPOON DRY MUSTARD

1 TABLESPOON FRESH LEMON JUICE

2 TEASPOONS STEAK SAUCE

1/2 POUND WHITE MUSHROOMS, TRIMMED,
WIPED CLEAN, AND THINLY SLICED

1 POUND CARROTS, TRIMMED, PEELED,
HALVED, AND CUT INTO 1-INCH PIECES

1 CUP GREEN PEAS

4 MEDIUM POTATOES, PEELED AND CUT
INTO 1/2-INCH CUBES

1 CUP WHIPPING CREAM

1. Melt 3 tablespoons butter in medium saucepan over medium-high heat. Stir
   in flour. Reduce heat to medium and whisk until well blended, about 3 to 5
   minutes.

2. Stir in Essence of Silver and Gold and bring to boil. Reduce heat and simmer
   until sauce is thickened and smooth, about 7 to 10 minutes, stirring often.
   Season to taste with salt and pepper. Remove from heat and keep warm.

3. Arrange sliced onions in bottom of baking dish. Cut 2 1/2 tablespoons butter
   into thin slices and distribute evenly over onions.

4. Preheat oven to 425°F. Rinse chicken and pat dry. Season with salt and
   pepper. Place on top of onions and sprinkle with 2 tablespoons champagne.
   Add basil, oregano, mustard, lemon juice, and steak sauce.

5. Arrange mushrooms, carrots, and peas on top of chicken. Top with thin slices of remaining butter. Sprinkle with 2 more tablespoons champagne.

6. Pour sauce over chicken and sprinkle with remaining champagne. Sink potato cubes into sauce, leaving them only slightly submerged. Cover dish tightly and bake until vegetables are soft and chicken is done, about 45 to 50 minutes. Uncover and cook until protruding bits of potato are lightly browned, about 10 more minutes.

7. Arrange chicken and vegetables on serving platter. Cover and keep warm. Boil cream in medium saucepan over high heat until reduced by half, 3 to 5 minutes. Add to pan juices and boil several minutes to reduce and thicken slightly. Pour over chicken and serve immediately.

Serves 4 to 6.

Essence of Silver and Gold

2 PIECES (1 POUND EACH) BOTTOM ROUND
 OF VEAL, BONED AND TIED
2 WHOLE CHICKEN BREASTS (ABOUT 1
 POUND EACH), BONE IN
4 POUNDS VEAL BONES
2 LEEKS, TRIMMED, WASHED THOROUGHLY,
 AND COARSELY CHOPPED
2 CELERY STALKS, THICKLY SLICED
2 MEDIUM CARROTS, HALVED AND THICKLY
 SLICED
3 TO 4 BRANCHES FRESH THYME (OR 2
 TEASPOONS DRIED)
2 BAY LEAVES
2 LARGE ONIONS, PEELED AND STUCK WITH
 2 WHOLE CLOVES
2 TEASPOONS SALT
20 WHOLE BLACK PEPPERCORNS
12 CUPS WATER
4 CUPS GOOD-QUALITY DRY WHITE WINE

1. Trim veal and chicken of any fat.
 Have butcher saw veal bones into
 3 to 4 large pieces. Combine all
 ingredients in large, nonreactive
 stockpot and bring to boil over
 medium-high heat. Simmer
 uncovered 2 to 3 hours or until
 liquid measures about 4 cups,
 periodically skimming off any
 residue that rises to the top.

2. Line large sieve or colander with
 double layer of cheesecloth and
 set inside large bowl. Carefully
 ladle in hot stock, discarding
 solids. Let stock cool to room
 temperature, then cover and
 refrigerate. Remove any fat that
 hardens on top.

 Makes about 4 cups.

Eggplant and Tomato Pie

6 EGGPLANTS, HALVED LENGTHWISE
4 LARGE BEEFSTEAK TOMATOES, EACH
 CUT INTO 6 SLICES
GRATED PARMESAN CHEESE
OLIVE OIL
FRESH LEMON OR LIME JUICE
PEPPER
FRESH BASIL LEAVES

1. Preheat oven to 375°F. Bake
 eggplant in baking dish until
 tender, 20 to 30 minutes. Remove
 and let stand 5 to 10 minutes.
 Slice eggplant about same
 thickness as tomatoes.

2. Layer eggplant, tomatoes, and
 grated cheese in baking dish.
 Drizzle with oil and lemon juice.
 Sprinkle with pepper and cover
 completely with basil leaves, as
 if it were pastry topping.

3. Bake 1 hour. Turn off oven and
 let pie stand in oven until ready
 to serve.

 Serves 4 to 6.

*Wash all fruits and
vegetables in cold water
to remove any chemicals,
but never soak or store
them in water; vitamins B
and C are easily lost. Dry
all fruits and vegetables
after washing.*

JOAN LUNDEN TELEVISION PERSONALITY

Spinach Salad with Raspberries and Papaya

2 TEASPOONS GRATED ORANGE PEEL

2 TABLESPOONS FRESH ORANGE JUICE

2 TABLESPOONS WHITE WINE VINEGAR

1 TEASPOON HONEY

2 TABLESPOONS CANOLA OR VEGETABLE OIL

SALT AND PEPPER

10-OUNCE PACKAGE FRESH SPINACH, COARSE STEMS REMOVED, RINSED AND SPUN DRY

1 CUP RASPBERRIES

1 PAPAYA (OR MANGO, OR 2 PEACHES OR NECTARINES), PEELED, SEEDED, AND SLICED

1. Whisk first five ingredients in large bowl with salt and pepper to taste.

2. Tear spinach into bite-size pieces. Add to dressing along with raspberries and toss salad gently.

3. Arrange 1/4 of papaya slices on each of four plates, and mound 1/4 of salad mixture next to papaya slices. If desired, add 3 cups cooked and cubed chicken breast.

Serves 4.

My two favorite fruits are raspberries and papayas. We combined the two flavors with a spinach salad to create a colorful, flavorful, vitamin-rich salad. Try adding some chicken to make this a light and healthy main dish.

Eggplant Parmesan

2 SMALL EGGPLANTS (ABOUT 2 POUNDS
    TOTAL)
NONSTICK VEGETABLE SPRAY
JUICE OF 1 LEMON
SALT AND PEPPER
1 1/2 CUPS TOMATO SAUCE

1/4 POUND NONFAT OR LOW-FAT
    MOZZARELLA CHEESE, COARSELY
    GRATED
1/4 CUP CHOPPED PARSLEY
1/3 CUP GRATED PARMESAN CHEESE

1. Peel eggplants and slice crosswise 1/4 inch thick. Arrange slices in one layer
   on cookie sheet sprayed with nonstick vegetable spray. Sprinkle with lemon
   juice and salt and pepper to taste. Bake 10 minutes, turn slices over and bake
   an additional 10 minutes or until golden.

2. Preheat oven to 400°F. Spread 2 tablespoons tomato sauce in bottom of 8-inch
   round quiche pan or pie pan. Arrange half the eggplant slices over sauce,
   overlapping slightly. Top eggplant with 1/2 of remaining tomato sauce, 1/2
   of mozzarella, 1/2 of parsley, and 1/2 of Parmesan cheese. Repeat with
   remaining ingredients and bake 30 minutes or until very hot and bubbly.
   The eggplant parmesan can be made ahead and reheated at 350°F for 30
   to 40 minutes.

Serves 4 to 6.

*I always thought eggplant
parmesan was fattening,
but this version proved me
wrong. Enjoy all the flavors
of this classic dish without
all the fat.*

$\mathcal{S}$HIRLEY MACLAINE   ACTRESS

Shirley's Favorite Chicken Mushroom Soup

1 YOUNG CHICKEN, ABOUT 3 TO 4 POUNDS
1 GARLIC CLOVE, CRUSHED
1 TEASPOON GROUND CORIANDER
1 TEASPOON COARSELY GROUND PEPPER

OIL FOR FRYING
1/4 POUND MUSHROOMS, SLICED
1 TEASPOON SOY SAUCE

1. Cook chicken in covered pot in water to cover until tender. Remove flesh and cut into small pieces. Reboil chicken bones about 2 hours in same water, covered. Strain stock.

2. Sauté garlic, coriander, and pepper in a little oil. Add mushrooms and chicken meat, including liver. Add 4 cups chicken stock and soy sauce; simmer 10 to 15 minutes. Stir well and serve.

Serves 4.

Store mushrooms unwashed and covered with a damp paper towel, then placed inside a brown paper bag. Refrigerate and use as soon as possible.

$\mathcal{B}$OB MATHIAS　　OLYMPIC CHAMPION — DECATHLON

Lasagna

1/2 POUND LASAGNA NOODLES	1 CUP GRATED PARMESAN CHEESE
10 OUNCES FRESH SPINACH	2 TABLESPOONS CHOPPED PARSLEY
2 TABLESPOONS OLIVE OIL	SALT AND PEPPER
1 MEDIUM ONION, CHOPPED	4 TO 5 CUPS SPAGHETTI SAUCE *(homemade or store bought)*
1 GARLIC CLOVE, MINCED	
1/2 POUND FIRM TOFU, MASHED	3/4 CUP SHREDDED MOZZARELLA CHEESE

1. Cook lasagna noodles, drain, and set aside. Wash, chop, and steam spinach lightly; set aside.

2. Heat olive oil in skillet. Add onion and garlic and sauté over medium heat until onion is translucent.

3. Mix tofu, Parmesan cheese, parsley, and salt and pepper. Stir in sautéed vegetables.

4. Preheat oven to 350°F. Grease 8 × 11-inch baking dish. Build layers, alternating noodles, tofu mixture, spinach, spaghetti sauce, and mozzarella cheese. Cover with foil and bake 40 minutes. Remove foil and bake another 10 minutes.

Serves 4.

Tofu is popular throughout the Orient, particularly in Japan. It has a bland, slightly nutty flavor and takes on the flavor of the food with which it's cooked. Tofu's texture is smooth and creamy yet firm enough to slice. Tofu can be sliced, diced, or mashed and used in a variety of dishes including stir-fry, soups, salads, and casseroles. It is available in Asian markets, health food stores, and most supermarkets.

JOHNNY MATHIS SINGER/ENTERTAINER

Shrimp and Crab au Gratin

1/4 CUP (1/2 STICK) BUTTER OR MARGARINE
1 TEASPOON SALT
1 TEASPOON GRANULATED GARLIC
1/2 CUP ALL-PURPOSE FLOUR
3 CUPS HOT MILK
1 CUP GRATED PARMESAN CHEESE
10 OUNCES CRABMEAT
10 OUNCES RAW SHRIMP, SHELLED AND CLEANED
1/2 CUP GRATED CHEDDAR CHEESE
1 TEASPOON PAPRIKA
ADDITIONAL GRATED CHEDDAR CHEESE

1. Melt butter in saucepan and add salt and garlic. Stir in flour until smooth. Gradually stir in hot milk. Stir in 1/2 cup Parmesan cheese until blended. Add shellfish (being sure crabmeat is free of shell) and Cheddar cheese. Bring to boil, then turn off heat.

2. Mix remaining 1/2 cup Parmesan cheese with paprika and sprinkle half the mixture evenly over bottom of au gratin dish. Stir shellfish mixture well, then turn into the dish. Sprinkle with remaining Parmesan cheese and Cheddar cheese. (At this point, mixture may be frozen or refrigerated until ready to use.)

3. Preheat oven to 325°F. Bake seafood 8 minutes or until cheese melts.

Serves 4 to 6.

Duck with Wild Rice

2 FRESH DUCKS, ABOUT 3 POUNDS EACH
SALT AND PEPPER
1/2 CUP CHOPPED ONION
1 GREEN BELL PEPPER, SLICED
2 TO 3 CELERY STALKS, COARSELY CHOPPED
3 CUPS WATER

1. Preheat oven to 325°F. Clean ducks. Rub with salt and pepper. Place in baking pan, breast side up. Add onion, bell pepper, celery, and water to pan.

2. Cover and roast 2 hours or until ducks are tender, basting occasionally. Serve on bed of wild rice.

Wild Rice

1 CUP WILD RICE
3 CUPS WATER
PINCH OF SALT

1. Wash rice under running water.

2. In saucepan, bring water to boil with pinch of salt.

3. Add rice and bring to a full boil. Reduce heat to a low simmer, cover, and cook for 20 to 25 minutes. Drain rice and toss with fork.

Serves 4.

Creole Gumbo

3 TABLESPOONS BUTTER OR MARGARINE
3 TABLESPOONS ALL-PURPOSE FLOUR
1/2 CUP CHOPPED ONION
1 GARLIC CLOVE, MINCED
16-OUNCE CAN TOMATOES, CUT UP
    (including juice)
2 CUPS WATER
1 1/2 CUPS CHOPPED GREEN BELL PEPPER
2 BAY LEAVES
1 TEASPOON DRIED OREGANO, CRUSHED
1 TEASPOON DRIED THYME, CRUSHED
1/2 TEASPOON SALT
1/2 TEASPOON HOT PEPPER SAUCE
10-OUNCE PACKAGE FROZEN CUT OKRA,
    THAWED
2 CANS (4 1/2 OUNCES EACH) SHRIMP,
    DRAINED AND CUT
7 1/2-OUNCE CAN CRABMEAT, DRAINED,
    CARTILAGE REMOVED
HOT COOKED RICE

1. Melt butter in large saucepan. Blend in flour and cook, stirring constantly, until mixture is golden brown.

2. Stir in onion and garlic, cook until onion is tender but not brown. Stir in undrained tomatoes, water, green pepper, bay leaves, oregano, thyme, salt, and hot pepper sauce. Bring to boil, reduce heat, and simmer, covered, 20 minutes.

3. Remove bay leaves and stir in okra. Bring mixture to boil, then stir in shrimp and crab and heat through. Serve gumbo over hot cooked rice in soup plates. (Traditionally rice is mounded in a heated soup plate and the gumbo spooned around it.)

Serves 6.

Lobster with Mustard Sauce

1 LIVE LOBSTER (ABOUT 2 POUNDS)
SALT AND PEPPER
1 1/2 CUPS WHIPPING CREAM
3 TABLESPOONS PREPARED MUSTARD
3 TABLESPOONS BUTTER
1 TABLESPOON DRAINED CAPERS
1 TABLESPOON CORNSTARCH
HOT COOKED RICE

1. Preheat oven to 400°F. Place lobster into stockpot of boiling water and cook 5 minutes. Drain. Sprinkle fleshy underside with salt and pepper. Butter large sheet of foil. Place lobster in center and wrap completely. Set in roasting pan and bake 45 minutes.

2. Mix cream with mustard, butter, capers, and cornstarch in saucepan. Season with salt and pepper. Stir constantly over medium heat until boiling. Remove from heat.

3. Cut lobster in half and serve with rice. Pour sauce over lobster.

Serves 2.

Lobster meat becomes tough if cooked at too high a temperature or for too long. Boiling too long will also make the meat dry. Whole lobster is usually cooked by dropping it into boiling water and simmering for 5 to 6 minutes per pound.

★ ☆ ☆ ☆ ☆ ☆ ☆ ☆ ☆ ☆ ☆ ☆ ☆ ☆ ☆ ☆ ☆ ☆ ★

Creamed Potatoes

3 LARGE POTATOES, PEELED AND THINLY
   SLICED (ABOUT 5 CUPS)
1 GARLIC CLOVE, PEELED
6 TABLESPOONS (3/4 STICK) BUTTER
PINCH OF NUTMEG
1 1/2 CUPS WHIPPING CREAM

1. Preheat oven to 450°F. Dry potato
   slices in cloth. Rub garlic around
   inside of baking dish. Butter dish
   well, using 1/3 of the butter, and
   layer potato slices in dish. Season
   each layer with salt and sprinkle
   top lightly with nutmeg.

2. Pour cream over potatoes. Dot
   surface with remaining butter.
   Bake 10 minutes. Reduce oven
   temperature to 350°F and bake
   1 hour longer.

   Serves 4.

Southern Corn Bread

1 1/2 CUPS YELLOW CORNMEAL
1/2 CUP ALL-PURPOSE FLOUR
1 TEASPOON BAKING SODA
1/2 TEASPOON SALT
1 1/2 CUPS BUTTERMILK
2 TABLESPOONS SOLID VEGETABLE
   SHORTENING, MELTED
1 EGG, BEATEN

1. Preheat oven to 400°F. Grease
   9-inch square baking pan.

2. Combine cornmeal, flour, baking
   soda, and salt. Add buttermilk,
   shortening, and egg; stir to blend.
   Pour into prepared pan. Bake until
   golden, about 20 minutes.

   Serves 6.

MARLEE MATLIN   ACTRESS

Noodle Kugel

3 BAGS (7 OUNCES EACH) MANISCHEWITZ
  MEDIUM NOODLES

1 CUP SUGAR

1 CUP PACKED BROWN SUGAR

1 CUP (2 STICKS) BUTTER

6 EGGS

1 CUP SOUR CREAM

8 OUNCES CREAM CHEESE, SOFTENED

1 TEASPOON VANILLA

1 1/2 TEASPOONS CINNAMON

1. Preheat oven to 350°F. Cook noodles as directed. Drain and set aside.

2. Combine remaining ingredients in large bowl and blend well. Place cooked
   noodles in 15 × 10-inch glass baking dish. Pour mixture over noodles,
   covering thoroughly. Bake 40 minutes. Sprinkle additional brown sugar
   on top of kugel and bake 10 more minutes. Let cool at least 10 minutes
   before serving.

Serves 6.

*M*ARY McFADDEN   **FASHION DESIGNER**

Green Beans with Walnuts

2 POUNDS FRESH GREEN BEANS, TRIMMED
7 OUNCES WALNUTS, CHOPPED
1/3 GARLIC CLOVE, MINCED
2 TABLESPOONS WHITE VINEGAR
5 SPRIGS CILANTRO, CHOPPED
PINCH OF RED CHILI POWDER
SALT AND PEPPER
POMEGRANATE SEEDS FOR DECORATION

1. Steam green beans until tender. Run beans under cold water to stop cooking and retain color. Drain well.
2. Coarsely chop walnuts in food processor.
3. Combine beans, walnuts, garlic, vinegar, cilantro, and chili powder in bowl. Mix well. Season with salt and pepper. Place beans in serving dish and garnish with pomegranate seeds.

Serves 4.

Nigozi

For Dough:

2 EGG YOLKS

PINCH OF SALT

14 TABLESPOONS (1 3/4 STICKS)
    UNSALTED MARGARINE, MELTED

SCANT 1 CUP SOUR CREAM

1/2 TEASPOON BAKING SODA

2 TABLESPOONS WHITE VINEGAR

1 TABLESPOON SUGAR

UNBLEACHED ALL-PURPOSE FLOUR

For Filling:

2 EGG WHITES

7 OUNCES WALNUTS, FINELY GROUND

1 CUP RAISINS

1 CUP SUGAR

CONFECTIONERS' SUGAR

1. For dough: Combine egg yolks, salt, margarine, sour cream, baking soda, vinegar, and sugar and mix well. Fold in enough flour to make soft but not sticky dough. Knead until smooth and elastic.

2. For filling: Whip egg whites until fluffy. Add walnuts, raisins, and sugar. Set aside.

3. Divide dough into 4 equal portions. Roll each portion into circle. Cut each circle into 8 triangles. Put a full tablespoon of filling on each triangle. Starting from outside of triangle, roll toward center. Take each end of rolled triangle and fold over to center.

4. Preheat oven to 350°F. Place triangles on lightly buttered cookie sheet and bake 25 minutes or until golden brown. Let cool; sprinkle with confectioners' sugar.

Makes 32.

DEBBIE MEYER
OLYMPIC CHAMPION—SWIMMING

Applesauce Cake

1 CUP (2 STICKS) BUTTER
2 CUPS SUGAR
2 EGGS
3 1/2 CUPS ALL-PURPOSE FLOUR
2 TEASPOONS BAKING SODA
2 TEASPOONS CINNAMON
1 TEASPOON NUTMEG
1/2 TEASPOON GROUND CLOVES
1/2 TEASPOON SALT
2 CUPS APPLESAUCE, HEATED TO BOILING
1 CUP RAISINS
1 CUP CHOPPED WALNUTS
CHERRIES

1. Preheat oven to 350°F. Grease 10-inch tube pan and line bottom with circle of wax paper. Cream butter, sugar, and 2 eggs in large bowl. Set aside. Sift together flour, baking soda, cinnamon, nutmeg, cloves, and salt. Mix into creamed ingredients.

2. Mix hot applesauce, raisins, and walnuts into mixture. Pour into tube pan and bake 45 minutes. Dot with cherries, return to oven, and bake 15 more minutes or until toothpick inserted in center comes out dry. Cool cake 10 minutes in pan, then turn out onto rack to cool completely.

Serves 10 to 12.

Tamale Pie

1 GARLIC CLOVE, CHOPPED
1 ONION, CHOPPED
VEGETABLE OIL
1 1/2 TO 2 POUNDS GROUND BEEF
1/2 TEASPOON BAKING POWDER
16-OUNCE CAN CREAM-STYLE CORN
8-OUNCE CAN TOMATO SAUCE
1 CUP YELLOW CORNMEAL
1 CUP MILK
5 TABLESPOONS CHILI POWDER, OR MORE TO TASTE

1. Sauté garlic and onion in small amount of oil. Add ground beef and brown. Drain excess fat.

2. Combine baking powder, creamed corn, tomato sauce, cornmeal, milk, and chili powder. Add meat mixture and blend well.

3. Preheat oven to 350°F. Pour mixture into 8 × 12-inch pan and bake 1 1/2 hours.

Serves 4 to 6.

JOHN NABER   OLYMPIC CHAMPION — SWIMMING

The Naber House Vegetable Soup

2 SOUP BONES

2 POUNDS BEEF STEW MEAT, CUT UP

2 BAY LEAVES

1 LARGE ONION, DICED

1 CELERY STALK, DICED *(including leaves)*

1 BUNCH CARROTS, SLICED

6 (OR MORE) RUSSET POTATOES, PEELED AND DICED

2 TO 4 CANS (28 OUNCES EACH) TOMATOES, INCLUDING JUICE *(I buy the style that is peeled and diced to save time)*

SALT AND PEPPER TO TASTE

1. Place soup bones and stew meat in large soup pot. Add just enough water to cover. Add bay leaves. Bring to boil, then reduce heat and simmer 4 hours.

2. Remove bones and bay leaves. Add all remaining ingredients and bring to boil over high heat, then reduce heat and simmer until vegetables are done. You cannot overcook this soup, so it's a great dish to serve when you don't know what time people will want to eat. Just keep the fire on very low and stir once in a while. This soup is especially good the next day, as it starts to thicken from the cooked vegetables.

Serves lots of people!

The Naber house serves this soup on New Year's Eve, as we can walk to the Rose Parade route and see the floats the night before the parade.

$\mathscr{L}$EROY NEIMAN   ARTIST

Terrific Turkey Pie

2 CUPS CUT-UP COOKED TURKEY
8 MUSHROOMS, SLICED
1/2 CUP SLICED GREEN ONIONS
1 CUP SHREDDED GRUYÈRE CHEESE
SALT AND PEPPER

1 1/2 CUPS MILK
3/4 CUP BISQUICK BAKING MIX
3 EGGS
PARSLEY FOR GARNISH

1. Preheat oven to 400°F. Lightly grease 10-inch pie pan or ceramic dish. Sprinkle turkey, mushrooms, green onions, and cheese into pan. Season with salt and pepper to taste.

2. Beat milk, Bisquick, and eggs until smooth (about 16 seconds in processor). Pour over ingredients in pie pan and bake until golden brown and knife inserted halfway between center and edge comes out clean, about 35 minutes. Let stand 5 minutes before cutting. Garnish with parsley.

A celebrated Swiss cheese from unpasteurized cow's milk, Gruyère is pale yellow and very firm and close-textured, with a sprinkling of small holes. It is sweet and nutty with a briny aftertaste. Gruyère is a wonderful dessert cheese and widely used in cooking, probably best known in the traditional Swiss cheese dish fondue. It is available at cheese shops and many supermarkets.

*M*ARK O'MEARA   GOLF CHAMPION

King Neptune Rolls

15 1/2-OUNCE CAN RED SALMON, DRAINED,
    BONES REMOVED

8 OUNCES CREAM CHEESE

2 TABLESPOONS CHOPPED ONION

1 TABLESPOON FRESH LEMON JUICE

2 TABLESPOONS CREAMED HORSERADISH

1/4 TEASPOON LIQUID SMOKE

1/4 TEASPOON LAWRY'S SEASONED SALT

5 DROPS TABASCO SAUCE

1 CUP CHOPPED PECANS OR WALNUTS

1 CUP CHOPPED PARSLEY

1. Combine salmon and cream cheese in bowl, mixing thoroughly. Add onion, lemon juice, horseradish, liquid smoke, seasoned salt, and Tabasco.
2. Combine nuts and parsley on large, flat plate.
3. Divide salmon mixture in half and form into 2 logs. Roll each log in nuts and parsley until covered. Wrap in plastic and refrigerate. Serve rolls at room temperature with your favorite crackers. The rolls can be made ahead and frozen for future use.

Makes 2 rolls.

⨍RNOLD PALMER   GOLF CHAMPION

Chili Salsa

2 POUNDS CHILI PEPPERS, PEELED,
  SEEDED, AND CHOPPED

5 POUNDS TOMATOES, PEELED, SEEDED,
  AND COARSELY CHOPPED

1 POUND ONIONS, PEELED AND
  COARSELY CHOPPED

1 CUP VINEGAR

1 TABLESPOON SALT

1/2 TEASPOON PEPPER

1. Preheat oven to 400°F. Use rubber gloves to handle chili peppers. Wash
   and dry peppers; slit side of each pepper to let steam escape. Place chilies
   on cookie sheet and bake 6 to 8 minutes. Remove from oven and let peppers
   cool. Remove skin and seeds; discard. Chop peppers.

2. Combine peppers, tomatoes, onions, vinegar, salt, and pepper and bring to
   boil. Simmer 10 minutes.

3. Cover and refrigerate until ready to use. Will keep refrigerated for up to
   3 days. Serve salsa at room temperature. Serve with chips, nachos, meats,
   or use as a condiment for your favorite foods.

   Makes about 10 cups.

**Seeding and Deveining
Fresh Chilies**
*Cut or break off the stems,
cut the chilies in half
lengthwise, then cut out the
veins and scoop out the
seeds. Make sure to wear
rubber gloves so that your
hands will not be burned
and you don't rub your
eyes. Chili peppers contain
an oil that will actually
burn your skin. You can
get relief by washing the
area with white vinegar.*

$\mathcal{J}$ACQUES PEPIN   CELEBRITY CHEF

Pasta with Fresh Vegetable Sauce

3 QUARTS WATER

1/2 POUND SPAGHETTI

1/4 CUP VIRGIN OLIVE OIL

1 LARGE RED ONION, PEELED AND THINLY SLICED (1 1/2 CUPS)

1 SMALL EGGPLANT (6 OUNCES), CUT INTO 1/2-INCH PIECES

3 TO 4 GARLIC CLOVES, FINELY CHOPPED (ABOUT 2 TEASPOONS)

2 RIPE TOMATOES, SEEDED AND CUT INTO 1/2-INCH PIECES

1 TEASPOON SALT

1/2 TEASPOON FRESHLY GROUND PEPPER

2 TABLESPOONS COARSELY CHOPPED PARSLEY

ABOUT 2 TABLESPOONS GRATED PARMESAN CHEESE

1. Bring water to a boil. Add pasta, return water to boil, and cook about 8 minutes or until pasta is al dente.

2. Meanwhile, heat oil in large saucepan and sauté onion and eggplant until soft and lightly browned, 6 to 7 minutes. Remove from heat and mix in garlic. Add tomatoes, salt, and pepper; mix thoroughly and set aside.

3. Remove 1/3 cup pasta cooking liquid and add to eggplant mixture. Drain pasta and add to saucepan, tossing to coat with vegetables.

4. Divide pasta and vegetables among four plates and sprinkle with parsley.

Serve with Parmesan cheese to taste.

*This recipe appears in *Jacques Pepin's Table*, KQED Books & Video, 1995.

Here's a low-calorie pasta dish that can be made in less than 20 minutes!

Omelette de Campagne

1 1/2 TABLESPOONS CANOLA OIL

1 TABLESPOON UNSALTED BUTTER

2 MEDIUM ONIONS (ABOUT 8 OUNCES), SLICED

3/4 POUND RAW POTATOES OR 2 MEDIUM BOILED POTATOES, PEELED AND THINLY SLICED

6 LARGE EGGS

1/3 CUP COARSELY CHOPPED CHIVES

1/2 TEASPOON SALT

1/4 TEASPOON FRESHLY GROUND PEPPER

1 TOMATO, THINLY SLICED

1. Heat oil and butter in broilerproof nonstick skillet until hot but not smoking. Add onions and potatoes and cook, covered, about 10 minutes if using raw potatoes or 5 minutes if using cooked potatoes, stirring occasionally.

2. Meanwhile, break eggs into bowl. Add chives, salt, and pepper and mix with fork. Reserve.

3. Add tomato slices to skillet, arranging them so they cover most of potato and onion mixture. Cover and cook 1 minute.

4. Preheat broiler. Add egg mixture to skillet and stir gently with fork for about 1 minute to allow eggs to flow between potatoes. Place skillet under broiler, about 3 to 4 inches from heat, and cook about 3 minutes or until eggs are set.

5. Invert omelette onto platter, cut into wedges, and serve.

Serves 4.

*This recipe appears in *Jacques Pepin's Kitchen: Cooking with Claudine*, KQED Books & Video, 1996.

*R*EGIS PHILBIN   TELEVISION HOST/ENTERTAINER

Joy's Perfect Bow-ties

1 POUND FARFALLE (BOW-TIE) PASTA

2 TABLESPOONS PLUS 1/4 CUP OLIVE OIL

2 GARLIC CLOVES, MINCED

2 BONELESS, SKINLESS CHICKEN BREASTS
(ABOUT 1/2 POUND EACH), CUT INTO
THIN STRIPS

2 CUPS BROCCOLI FLORETS

1 CUP OIL-PACKED SUN-DRIED TOMATOES,
DRAINED AND SLICED

2 TABLESPOONS CHOPPED FRESH BASIL

PINCH OF RED PEPPER FLAKES

1/4 CUP DRY WHITE WINE

3/4 CUP CHICKEN STOCK

SALT AND PEPPER

1 TABLESPOON UNSALTED BUTTER

FRESHLY GRATED PARMESAN CHEESE

1. Cook pasta according to package directions. Drain well and place in large mixing bowl. Pour 2 tablespoons olive oil over pasta and stir to coat and separate. Set aside.

2. Pour remaining olive oil into large skillet or saucepan set over medium-high heat. Add garlic and cook until slightly softened, about 1 minute. Add chicken and cook thoroughly, about 5 minutes, turning occasionally. Transfer chicken to plate, cover with foil to keep warm, and set aside.

3. Reduce heat to low and add broccoli to pan. Stir and toss until broccoli is tender, about 10 minutes. Return chicken to pan and add sun-dried tomatoes, basil, red pepper flakes, wine, and chicken stock. Season to taste with salt and pepper. Add butter, cover, and simmer on low 5 minutes.

4. Add chicken and broccoli mixture to cooked pasta and toss to blend. Serve at once with lots of grated Parmesan cheese on the side.

Serves 4.

$\mathscr{M}$ICHELLE PHILLIPS ACTRESS/SINGER

Shrimp and Feta

1 DOZEN FRESH SHRIMP, SHELLED AND
  DEVEINED, TAILS ON
1/2 CUP VIRGIN OLIVE OIL
1/2 CUP CRUMBLED FETA CHEESE

1/4 CUP FRESH LIME JUICE
1/4 CUP MINCED FRESH MINT

1. Grill shrimp 2 to 3 minutes or until done.
2. Combine all remaining ingredients and pour over shrimp in shallow serving
   dish. Refrigerate 2 hours. Serve cold.

   Serves 2.

Feta is a classic Greek cheese traditionally made of sheep's or goat's milk. The cheese is white and crumbly and has a rich, tangy flavor. Feta makes a zesty addition to salads and other cooked dishes. It's available at Greek markets, cheese shops, and many supermarkets.

STEFANIE POWERS ACTRESS

Pierogi

For Dough:

2 1/2 POUNDS (ABOUT 10 CUPS)
   ALL-PURPOSE FLOUR

4 EGGS

16-OUNCE CONTAINER SOUR CREAM

SALT

1. Mix flour, eggs, sour cream, salt, and enough warm water to make firm dough. Knead in bowl, cover with towel, and let stand 10 minutes. Prepare filling.

For Filling:

2 LARGE POTATOES, BOILED, DRAINED, AND MASHED

1/2 CUP (1 STICK) BUTTER OR MARGARINE

2 POUNDS POT OR HOOP CHEESE

3 EGGS, BEATEN

SALT AND PEPPER

2. Mix ingredients together well.

3. To assemble the pierogi, knead dough until smooth. Roll out dough until thin. Cut into 3-inch squares or 3-inch rounds. Place 1 teaspoon of filling in center of each square or round and fold dough in half to make a triangle or half circle. Pinch edges well to keep pierogi from falling apart.

4. To cook, drop pierogi into large pot of boiling salted water and cook, covered, until they float to the top, about 10 to 15 minutes. Drain and place on heated platter. Drizzle with melted butter and sprinkle with bread crumbs.

Serves 4 to 6.

Pot cheese is similar to cottage cheese, but is drier and never creamed. It is usually made without salt and additives.

★ ☆ ★ ☆ ★ ☆ ★ ☆ ★ ☆ ★ ☆ ★ ☆ ★ ☆ ★ ☆ ★ ☆ ★

SALLY JESSY RAPHAEL

TELEVISION TALK SHOW HOST

Baked French Toast

1 LOAF WHITE BREAD, CUBED
8 OUNCES CREAM CHEESE, CUBED
8 TO 12 EGGS, DEPENDING ON SIZE

1/2 CUP MAPLE SYRUP
1 CUP MILK

1. Line bottom of 11 × 13-inch pan with 1/2 the bread cubes. Next, layer cream cheese on top of bread. Cover with remaining bread cubes.

2. Beat eggs, maple syrup, and milk together. Pour mixture over bread. Cover and refrigerate overnight.

3. Preheat oven to 350°F. Bake French toast 45 minutes or until light golden brown.

Serves 8.

As served at the Isaac Stover House, owned by award-winning talk show host Sally Jessy Raphael.

*N*ANCY REAGAN   FORMER FIRST LADY

Monkey Bread

1 ENVELOPE DRY YEAST
1 TO 1 1/4 CUPS WARM MILK
3 EGGS
3 TABLESPOONS SUGAR
1 TEASPOON SALT

3 1/2 CUPS ALL-PURPOSE FLOUR
12 TABLESPOONS (1 1/2 STICKS) BUTTER, AT ROOM TEMPERATURE
1 CUP (2 STICKS) BUTTER, MELTED
TWO 9-INCH RING MOLDS

1. In bowl, mix yeast with some of milk until dissolved. Beat in 2 eggs. Mix in dry ingredients. Add remaining milk a little at a time, mixing thoroughly. Cut in room-temperature butter until blended.

2. Knead dough until smooth and elastic. Let rise 1 to 1 1/2 hours or until doubled in size. Knead again and let rise 40 minutes.

3. Roll out dough on floured board and shape into log. Cut into 28 equal pieces. Shape each piece into ball and roll in melted butter.

4. Place 7 balls in each mold, leaving space between. Place remaining balls on top, spacing evenly. Let dough rise in molds until doubled, about 45 to 60 minutes.

5. Preheat oven to 375°F. Brush tops of loaves with remaining beaten egg. Bake approximately 15 minutes or until golden brown.

$\mathcal{K}$IM RHODE   OLYMPIC CHAMPION—SHOOTING

Fish Gumbo

12- TO 18-INCH FISH OF YOUR CHOICE

4 SLICES BACON

1 LARGE ONION, DICED

1 LARGE POTATO, THINLY SLICED

15-OUNCE CAN OKRA, DRAINED, JUICE RESERVED

15-OUNCE CAN TOMATOES, MASHED

4-OUNCE CAN TOMATO SAUCE

3 OR 4 WHOLE CLOVES

SCHILLING SHRIMP SPICE

SALT AND PEPPER

8-OUNCE BOTTLE CLAM JUICE

10 1/2-OUNCE CAN VEGETARIAN VEGETABLE SOUP

COOKED RICE

1. Fillet the fish, removing head, tail, skin, and bones. Cut fish into bite-size cubes and refrigerate. Place fish head, tail, and bones in saucepan, cover with water, bring to boil, and simmer 2 hours. Strain fish broth and set aside.

2. Fry bacon in large stockpot. Remove bacon, add onion and potato to pot and sauté until onion is clear and potato nearly done. Add okra, tomatoes, tomato sauce, whole cloves, and fish broth. Season to taste with shrimp spice and salt and pepper. Cover and simmer 30 minutes.

3. Add clam juice, vegetable soup, juice from okra, and cubed raw fish and simmer an additional 15 minutes. Serve over steamed white rice.

Serves 4.

GERALDO RIVERA

TELEVISION PERSONALITY/JOURNALIST

Green Banana Salad

10 GREEN BANANAS, PEELED
2 ENVELOPES SAZON SEASONING
2 ROASTED RED BELL PEPPERS, SEEDED
   AND CUT INTO PIECES
12 STUFFED OLIVES
A FEW DROPS WHITE VINEGAR
1 TABLESPOON OLIVE OIL
1 TABLESPOON VEGETABLE OIL
1 MEDIUM ONION, SLICED
2 BAY LEAVES

1. Boil green bananas in water to
   cover until tender but not mushy,
   about 20 to 25 minutes. Place
   bananas in cold water to cool.
   Cut into 1/4-inch slices.

2. Mix all remaining ingredients and
   toss with bananas. Serve at room
   temperature.

   Serves 6 to 8.

Amaretto Caramel Custard

1 CUP SUGAR
14-OUNCE CAN CONDENSED MILK
12-OUNCE CAN EVAPORATED MILK
4 LARGE EGGS
1 CUP WATER
1/2 CUP AMARETTO LIQUEUR

1. To prepare caramel, place sugar
   in metal bowl over medium heat.
   Stir until melted (do not burn)
   and let cool.

2. Mix all remaining ingredients and
   place in caramel bowl. Set bowl
   over pot of simmering water and
   cook on low heat until knife
   inserted in center comes out clean.
   Cool and chill 2 hours before
   serving.

   Serves 8 to 10.

*Amaretto is a liqueur with
the flavor of almonds. The
original liqueur, Amaretto
di Saronno, comes from
Saronno, Italy. Various
brands are available at
most supermarkets and
liquor stores.*

$\mathscr{J}$OAN RIVERS   COMEDIENNE/ENTERTAINER

Joan Rivers's Toast

2 SLICES WHITE BREAD*
BUTTER OR MARGARINE

1. Take two slices of white bread. Place them in a toaster and press down the handle. Wait two minutes or until toast pops up.
2. Spread butter over slices *after* removing them from the toaster.

Serves 2.

*For holidays and special occasions, raisin bread may be substituted, but follow the same procedure as above. For these special occasions we call it "Joan Rivers's Holiday Toast."

This recipe has been in my family for generations.

$\mathcal{K}$ENNY ROGERS   SINGER/SONGWRITER/ACTOR

Chicken Salad à la Rogers

2 CUPS COOKED WHITE MEAT CHICKEN 1/4 CUP CHOPPED ALMONDS
3 DILL PICKLES CHOPPED GREEN ONIONS (OPTIONAL)
1/2 CUP CHOPPED WALNUTS LETTUCE LEAVES

1. Pull chicken from bone rather than cutting it. Peel pickles with potato peeler; chop.
2. Mix all ingredients lightly with dressing of your choice. Season to taste and serve on a bed of crisp lettuce.

I'm pleased to share one of my very favorite recipes with you. This is a delicious recipe for luncheons and light suppers. Guests love it as well. Happy eating!

$\mathscr{L}$INDA RONSTADT SINGER

Corn Muffins

1 CUP WHOLE-WHEAT FLOUR
1 CUP YELLOW CORNMEAL
4 TEASPOONS BAKING POWDER
1/2 TEASPOON SALT
1/4 CUP SUGAR

2 EGGS, LIGHTLY BEATEN
1 CUP NONFAT MILK
3 TABLESPOONS BUTTER, MELTED
1 CUP CREAM-STYLE CORN

1. Preheat oven to 425°F. Grease 12 muffin cups. Combine first five ingredients in large bowl. Combine eggs, milk, butter, and corn in medium bowl. Add to dry mixture, stirring until dry ingredients are moistened.

2. Spoon batter into prepared muffin cups. Bake 20 to 25 minutes or until tops are golden. Serve warm.

Makes 12.

PAT SAJAK TELEVISION GAME SHOW HOST/ENTERTAINER

Gin Fizz Egg Pie

6 STRIPS THICK BACON
1 ONION, DICED
28-OUNCE CAN PEELED TOMATOES
10 FRESH MUSHROOMS, SLICED
2 CANS VIENNA SAUSAGES, CUT INTO
   1/4-INCH SLICES
6 SLICES AMERICAN OR JACK CHEESE

1 DOZEN EGGS
1/2 CUP WHIPPING CREAM
PARMESAN CHEESE
PIMIENTO STRIPS
SOUR CREAM
A SHAKER OF GIN FIZZES

1. Cut bacon into 1-inch pieces and fry in large ovenproof skillet until crisp.
   Pour off most of fat. Brown onion in remaining fat.

2. Mix in tomatoes, mushrooms, and Vienna sausages and simmer 15 minutes,
   adding cheese slices during last minute.

3. Preheat oven to 350°F. Gently beat eggs with cream and stir into pan
   mixture. Bake 30 minutes or until eggs have cooked to nice golden crust,
   sprinkling Parmesan cheese over crust during last 5 minutes of baking.

Serves 6 to 8.

Serving suggestions:

Mix a shaker of gin fizzes after putting pan into oven and enjoy until eggs are
done. Serve pie in slices, garnished with thin strips of pimiento on each slice and
a bowl of sour cream on the side for those who wish this final touch.

*Try this classic Gin Fizz recipe.
Here's looking at you, kid!*
  *3 ounces (6 tablespoons) gin
  1 tablespoon superfine sugar
  2 tablespoons fresh lemon juice
  1 tablespoon fresh lime juice
  3 or 4 ice cubes
  Club soda*
*Combine all ingredients except
club soda in cocktail shaker and
shake vigorously. Strain into
highball glass and fill with club
soda. Serves 1.*

CONNIE SELLECCA   ACTRESS

Penne con Broccoli

2 TABLESPOONS OLIVE OIL
6 TO 8 GARLIC CLOVES, SLICED
1/4 CUP (1/2 STICK) BUTTER
1 1/2 TO 2 CUPS GRATED PARMESAN CHEESE
3/4 TO 1 CUP TOMATO SAUCE
1 TO 1 1/2 CUPS SLICED MUSHROOMS

2 ROMA TOMATOES, CHOPPED
2 CUPS BROCCOLI, COOKED AL DENTE
1 CUP RAISINS
1/2 TO 3/4 CUP PINE NUTS
SALT AND PEPPER
1 POUND PENNE PASTA, COOKED AL DENTE

1. Heat olive oil in large skillet and sauté garlic briefly. Add butter. When melted, slowly add Parmesan cheese, stirring constantly over low heat to get thick, soupy consistency. Add tomato sauce over low to medium heat.

2. Add mushrooms and Roma tomatoes and cook until tender but not too soft. If desired, add more cheese and/or tomato sauce to thicken or thin sauce to your taste.

3. Add broccoli, raisins, and pine nuts and simmer slowly 5 minutes. Season with salt and pepper. Pour sauce over cooked penne and serve.

Serves 6.

Al dente *is literally the Italian phrase for "to the tooth." It is used to describe the texture of food, especially pasta, when it is properly cooked but just firm to the bite. The term also refers to vegetables.*

*R*ED SKELTON **COMEDIAN**

Ham Hock and Lima Beans

1 POUND DRIED LARGE WHITE LIMA BEANS
1 LARGE ONION, DICED
2 LARGE CELERY STALKS, DICED
2 LARGE CARROTS, DICED

2 WHOLE PEPPERCORNS
1 TEASPOON SALT
PINCH OF NUTMEG
1 GOOD-SIZED SMOKED HAM HOCK, WASHED

1. Place lima beans in large bowl and cover completely with water. Let stand overnight. Drain, reserving soaking water.
2. Place lima beans in good-sized pot. Add 1/2 of soaking water and cook, covered, over low heat 15 minutes.
3. Add onion, celery, carrots, peppercorns, salt, and nutmeg and simmer another 15 minutes.
4. Add ham hock and simmer 1 hour, adding more bean-soaking water if necessary. Important to this recipe: Do not overseason! Remember that the smoked ham hock is highly seasoned and will add spice to the recipe.

Serves 4.

The ham hock is the lower portion of a hog's leg, made up of meat, fat, bone, and gristle. In supermarkets, ham hocks are usually cut into 2- to 3-inch lengths. Most have been cured, smoked, or both. Fresh ones can sometimes be found at butcher shops. Ham hocks are used to flavor beans, soups, and stews that require slow, lengthy cooking.

$\mathscr{K}$EVIN SORBO ACTOR

Caramel Corn

1/2 CUP POPCORN KERNELS
1/4 CUP (1/2 STICK) BUTTER
1/2 CUP PACKED BROWN SUGAR
1/2 CUP LIGHT CORN SYRUP
1/4 TEASPOON VANILLA

1. Pop corn by your preferred method. Place in large mixing bowl and set aside.
2. Melt butter in saucepan. Add brown sugar and melt to soft bubbles. Add corn syrup and boil gently 2 to 3 minutes. Add vanilla and stir 1 minute.
3. Pour caramel mixture over popcorn and mix with wooden spoon.

Makes approximately 4 cups.

I make this on late nights when an old movie favorite is on the tube. Can't beat the combo!

OLIVER STONE

MOTION PICTURE DIRECTOR/SCREENWRITER

Miriam Jimenez's Salvadoran Chicken

1/4 GREEN BELL PEPPER, SEEDED
1/4 RED BELL PEPPER, SEEDED
1/2 ONION
1 TOMATO
4 GARLIC CLOVES, PEELED
1/2 TEASPOON SESAME SEEDS
1 TEASPOON PEPITAS (ROASTED HULLED PUMPKIN SEEDS)
1 CUP WATER

1/2 TEASPOON SALT
MAGGI SEASONING
1 PASILLA CHILI *(available at Latino markets)*
1 GUACA CHILI *(available at Latino markets)*
1/2 TEASPOON PAPRIKA
OLIVE OIL
10 SKINLESS, BONELESS CHICKEN BREASTS
BABY CARROTS, BABY ZUCCHINI, AND GREEN BEANS

1. Combine first 13 ingredients in blender and puree.
2. Heat small amount of olive oil in large saucepan over medium heat. Add puree and simmer 10 minutes. Add chicken and simmer 10 minutes. Add carrots, zucchini, and green beans and cook 5 minutes. Serve chicken breast with vegetables on side.

Serves 6.

Pepitas are pumpkin seeds, a popular ingredient in Mexican cooking. With their white hull removed, they are a medium-dark green and have a delicate flavor. Pepitas are sold salted, roasted, and raw, with or without hulls. Stored in the freezer and well wrapped, pepitas will last 6 months or more. They are available in health food stores, Mexican markets, and many supermarkets.

★ ★ ★ ★ ★ ★ ★ ★ ★ ★ ★ ★ ★ ★ ★ ★ ★ ★ ★ ★

JPS Tomato Salad

8 RIPE TOMATOES, CUT INTO 1/4-INCH SLICES
1/2 ONION, FINELY CHOPPED
1 BUNCH PARSLEY, FINELY CHOPPED
2 HARD-BOILED EGGS, FINELY CHOPPED
3 TABLESPOONS OLIVE OIL
2 TEASPOONS RED WINE VINEGAR
1/2 TEASPOON PEPPER
1 TABLESPOON DIJON MUSTARD
PINCH OF SALT

1. Arrange layer of sliced tomatoes on platter. Mix all remaining ingredients for dressing and let stand 1 hour.

2. Pour dressing over tomatoes 15 minutes before serving.

   Serves 4.

*K*ERRI STRUG OLYMPIC CHAMPION—GYMNASTICS

Nonfat Zucchini Bread

3 CUPS ALL-PURPOSE FLOUR

1 TABLESPOON CINNAMON

1 TEASPOON LITE SALT

1 TEASPOON BAKING POWDER

1 TEASPOON BAKING SODA

3/4 CUP EGG BEATERS, BEATEN

1 CUP SUGAR

1 CUP PACKED BROWN SUGAR

1 CUP LIQUID BUTTER BUDS OR FAT-FREE MARGARINE

2 TEASPOONS VANILLA

2 CUPS GRATED MIXED ZUCCHINI AND CARROTS

1. Preheat oven to 350°F. Spray two 9 × 5-inch loaf pans with nonfat vegetable spray. Sift together flour, cinnamon, salt, baking powder, and baking soda. Set aside.

2. In another bowl mix Egg Beaters, sugar, brown sugar, Butter Buds, and vanilla. Add sifted ingredients and blend in grated zucchini and carrots.

3. Pour batter into loaf pans and bake 65 minutes or until knife inserted in center comes out clean.

Makes 2 loaves.

$\mathcal{D}$AVE THOMAS CHAIRMAN, WENDY'S INTERNATIONAL

Dave's Favorite Pasta

14 ROMA TOMATOES, CHOPPED

4 GARLIC CLOVES, CHOPPED

2 TABLESPOONS CHOPPED FRESH BASIL

2 TABLESPOONS OLIVE OIL

2 TABLESPOONS FAT-FREE CHICKEN BROTH
OR VEGETABLE BROTH

2 TABLESPOONS RED WINE VINEGAR

6-OUNCE PACKAGE ANGEL HAIR PASTA

1 TABLESPOON FAT-FREE CHICKEN BROTH

6 TO 8 MUSHROOMS, SLICED

SALT AND PEPPER

FAT-FREE PARMESAN CHEESE

1. Combine tomatoes, garlic, basil, olive oil, 2 tablespoons broth, and vinegar in bowl and let stand at room temperature at least 2 hours. Tomato mixture should be room temperature; if not room temperature, microwave briefly but do not cook.

2. Boil pasta in water and 1 tablespoon chicken broth until al dente.

3. Arrange mushroom slices on cookie sheet, spray lightly with vegetable oil spray, and broil for a few minutes. Turn mushrooms; spray and broil again.

4. Drain pasta and toss immediately with tomato mixture. Spoon mushrooms on top. Sprinkle with salt and pepper and Parmesan cheese.

Serves 2.

This is a very easy and healthful pasta dish. I like to add sliced red pepper and onion to the pasta as well.

CHERYL TIEGS   ACTRESS/MODEL

Nonfat Chunky Gazpacho

3 POUNDS (ABOUT 8 LARGE) RIPE
TOMATOES, PEELED, SEEDED, AND
COARSELY CHOPPED, JUICES RESERVED

1 LARGE CUCUMBER, PEELED AND DICED
(you may remove seeds if you like)

1/2 CUP DICED ONION

1/2 CUP DICED GREEN BELL PEPPER

1/2 CUP DICED RED BELL PEPPER

2 WHOLE GREEN ONIONS, TRIMMED AND
THINLY SLICED

3 GARLIC CLOVES, MINCED

2 TABLESPOONS RED WINE VINEGAR

2 TABLESPOONS DRY SHERRY OR SHERRY
VINEGAR

SALT AND PEPPER

1 TO 1 1/2 CUPS CHILLED TOMATO JUICE

1 TO 2 TEASPOONS HOT PEPPER SAUCE
(OPTIONAL)

AVOCADO SLICES (OPTIONAL)

MINCED FRESH HERBS, SUCH AS CILANTRO
OR CHIVES (OPTIONAL)

1. Stir together tomatoes and juices, cucumber, onion, bell peppers, green onions, and garlic in large bowl or pitcher. When blended, add vinegar, sherry, and salt and pepper to taste.

2. Stir in just enough tomato juice to make soup liquid but not soupy. Add hot sauce and adjust seasonings to taste.

3. Cover and chill for at least a day—two is even better. If necessary, add more cold tomato juice to reach consistency you wish. Serve cold, garnished with avocado slices and herbs, if desired.

Serves 4 to 6.

To peel tomatoes easily, place them in boiling water, remove from heat, and allow to stand 1 minute. Then plunge them into cold water. The skin will peel off without difficulty. Another way to peel a tomato is to place a long fork into it and hold it over a gas burner until the skin blisters.

★ ★ ★ ★ ★ ★ ★ ★ ★ ★ ★ ★ ★ ★ ★ ★ ★ ★ ★ ★

New Potato Salad in Mustard Vinaigrette

2 POUNDS SMALL RED POTATOES *(buy the tiniest ones you can find)*, WASHED

1/4 CUP RED WINE VINEGAR

1/4 CUP EXTRA VIRGIN OLIVE OIL

1 TABLESPOON DIJON MUSTARD

3 TABLESPOONS CHOPPED FRESH CHIVES

1 TABLESPOON CHOPPED FLAT-LEAF PARSLEY

1 TEASPOON SALT

PEPPER

1. Place potatoes in large saucepan and add cold water to cover by 2 to 3 inches. Bring to boil over medium-high heat. Reduce heat to low, cover, and simmer 15 to 20 minutes or until fork tender but not falling apart. Drain potatoes and set aside until just cool enough to handle.

2. Meanwhile, combine all remaining ingredients in jar. Cover and shake well. Taste and adjust seasonings.

3. When potatoes are cool enough to handle, peel, if desired. Quarter each potato and place in large mixing bowl. Shake vinaigrette again and pour over warm potatoes. Gently toss or fold until potatoes are coated with vinaigrette. Serve warm or cover and chill, tossing occasionally.

Serves 4 to 6.

DONALD TRUMP   BUSINESSMAN

Lemon Chicken

1 CHICKEN, ABOUT 3 1/2 POUNDS	4 YELLOW ONIONS, HALVED CROSSWISE
2 TEASPOONS DRIED TARRAGON	2 TABLESPOONS BALSAMIC VINEGAR
3 LEMONS	1/2 CUP CHICKEN STOCK
1/4 CUP (1/2 STICK) UNSALTED BUTTER	SALT AND PEPPER
2 TABLESPOONS DIJON MUSTARD	1 BUNCH WATERCRESS

1. Preheat oven to 375°F. Trim any excess fat from chicken. Sprinkle cavity with 1 teaspoon tarragon. Cut 1 lemon in half and place lemon half in cavity. Squeeze remaining lemons to make 1/4 cup juice.

2. Melt butter in small pan over medium heat. Stir in lemon juice, remaining 1 teaspoon tarragon and mustard; mix well. Brush some of butter mixture over surface of chicken. Place breast side down in shallow roasting pan. Arrange onions around chicken; brush 1/2 of remaining butter mixture over onions. Roast 30 minutes.

3. Spoon vinegar over onions and stir chicken stock into pan. Baste chicken with pan juices and roast another 30 minutes.

4. Turn chicken breast side up, baste with remaining butter mixture, and season with salt and pepper. Continue to roast until chicken is tender and golden, about 20 to 30 minutes.

5. Make bed of watercress on warmed platter. Place chicken on top and surround with onions. Baste chicken with some of pan juices; serve remaining juices on the side. Carve chicken at the table.

Serves 4.

Wonderfully dark and mellow, with a sweet-sour flavor, balsamic vinegar is made only in and around Modena in northern Italy. The vinegar is made from grape juice concentrated over a low flame and fermented slowly in a series of wooden barrels, beginning with large chestnut or oak barrels and moving each year into progressively smaller barrels in a variety of different woods. Balsamic vinegar is expensive, but a little goes a long way. It is available at Italian markets, gourmet food shops, and many supermarkets.

*T*ED TURNER BUSINESSMAN/PHILANTHROPIST

Karen's Pizza Dough

1 TEASPOON HONEY
1 CUP LUKEWARM WATER
2 TEASPOONS DRY YEAST
2 TABLESPOONS OLIVE OIL

1 TEASPOON SALT
1 1/2 CUPS SEMOLINA FLOUR
1 1/2 CUPS WHOLE-WHEAT FLOUR

1. Combine honey and water in food processor fitted with metal blade or in large bowl. Add yeast and let stand 5 minutes. Add oil, salt, and flours and process or mix until dough forms ball, about 30 seconds by machine or 5 minutes by hand.

2. Turn dough out onto lightly floured work surface and knead until smooth and elastic, about 5 minutes.

3. Coat large bowl with nonstick vegetable spray, add dough, and turn to coat all sides. Cover with plastic wrap and let rise in warm, draft-free place until doubled, about 1 hour.

4. Return dough to lightly floured work surface and, using your fist, punch down, then knead 2 minutes. Return to bowl, cover with plastic wrap, and let rise again for 30 minutes.

Makes one pound.

Semolina is a grainy, creamy-yellow flour ground from durum or hard wheat that has a higher protein and gluten content than flour produced from soft wheat. It is the main ingredient of dried pasta. Because it's hard flour to work by hand, it is nearly impossible to make pasta at home using only semolina. Try combining it with bread flour, using just one part semolina to two parts bread flour. Semolina is also used to make gnocchi, puddings, and cookies.

Ted's Favorite Pizza

1 ONION, CHOPPED

2 GARLIC CLOVES, MINCED

8 OUNCES GROUND BISON OR LEAN GROUND BEEF

1 TABLESPOON HERBES DE PROVENCE

8 OUNCES MUSHROOMS, SLICED

2 POUNDS ROMA TOMATOES, PEELED, SEEDED, AND DICED

1 TEASPOON SALT

1/2 TEASPOON PEPPER

1/4 CUP GRATED PARMESAN CHEESE

1 POUND KAREN'S PIZZA DOUGH *(see recipe on page 123)*

1 CUP SHREDDED LOW-FAT MOZZARELLA CHEESE

1. Preheat oven to 425°F. Coat large cookie sheet with nonstick vegetable spray.

2. Coat large nonstick skillet with nonstick spray and place over medium heat. Add onion and garlic and sauté 2 minutes. Add meat and herbs and sauté until meat is no longer pink, about 5 minutes for bison and 7 minutes for beef.

3. Add mushrooms, tomatoes, salt, and pepper and simmer until liquid evaporates, about 10 minutes. Remove from heat and stir in Parmesan cheese.

4. Roll out pizza dough on lightly floured work surface, into 12-inch round. Place on prepared cookie sheet and form 1/2-inch raised lip around edge. Top with meat mixture and mozzarella cheese, leaving 1/2-inch border around edge.

5. Bake until crust is golden and cheese is bubbly, about 15 minutes. To serve, slice into quarters and place on individual plates.

Serves 4.

Bison or buffalo meat is surprisingly tender, tastes somewhat like lean beef, and has no pronounced gamey flavor. Cuts are similar to beef and can be substituted for beef in many recipes. Buffalo is higher in iron than beef and lower in fat and cholesterol than most cuts of beef and chicken. It is becoming more widely available and can be found in some specialty meat markets.

★ ★

ABIGAIL (DEAR ABBY) VAN BUREN
NEWSPAPER COLUMNIST

Abby's Famous Pecan Pie

1 CUP LIGHT CORN SYRUP

1 CUP PACKED DARK BROWN SUGAR

3 EGGS, SLIGHTLY BEATEN

1/3 CUP BUTTER, MELTED

1/3 TEASPOON SALT

1 TEASPOON VANILLA

9-INCH UNBAKED PIE CRUST

1 GENEROUS CUP PECAN HALVES

1. Preheat oven to 350°F. Combine corn syrup, brown sugar, eggs, butter, salt, and vanilla in large bowl and mix well. Pour filling into prepared pie crust; sprinkle with pecan halves.

2. Bake 45 to 50 minutes or until center is set. (Toothpick inserted in center will come out clean when pie is done.) If crust or pie appears to be getting too brown, cover with foil for remaining baking time. Let cool.

3. You can top the pie with a bit of whipped cream or ice cream, but even plain—nothing tops this!

BETTY WHITE   ACTRESS/COMEDIENNE

Mandarin Salad

For Dressing:

1/2 TEASPOON SALT
1/4 TEASPOON PEPPER
2 TABLESPOONS SUGAR
2 TABLESPOONS VINEGAR

1/4 CUP VEGETABLE OIL
DASH OF HOT SAUCE
1 TABLESPOON CHOPPED PARSLEY

Combine all ingredients in jar and refrigerate until ready to use.

For Caramelized Almonds (this can be done ahead):

1/4 CUP SLICED ALMONDS
4 TEASPOONS SUGAR

1. Cook almonds and sugar over low heat, stirring constantly, until sugar is melted and almonds are coated.
2. Scrape out onto waxed paper and cool. Break apart and store at room temperature.

★ ★ ★ ★ ★ ★ ★ ★ ★ ★ ★ ★ ★ ★ ★ ★ ★ ★ ★

For Salad:

1/4 HEAD RED LEAF LETTUCE, TORN IN PIECES

1/4 HEAD ROMAINE LETTUCE, TORN IN PIECES

1 HEAD BUTTER LETTUCE, TORN IN PIECES

2 CELERY STALKS, SLICED

2 GREEN ONIONS WITH TOPS, THINLY SLICED

15-OUNCE CAN MANDARIN ORANGES, DRAINED

Just before serving, combine greens, celery, green onion, orange segments, almonds, and dressing. Toss to mix.

Serves 6.

To prevent soggy salads, place an inverted saucer in the bottom of the salad bowl. The excess liquid drains off under the saucer, and the salad stays fresh and crisp.

★ ★

$\mathcal{V}$ANNA WHITE TELEVISION PERSONALITY/ENTERTAINER

Cottage Cheese Salad

32-OUNCE CARTON PLAIN COTTAGE CHEESE
3-OUNCE PACKAGE LIME JELL-O
8-OUNCE CAN CRUSHED PINEAPPLE
  (in its own juice), DRAINED
8-OUNCE CONTAINER COOL WHIP TOPPING
  (REGULAR OR LITE)

1. Put cottage cheese in mixing bowl. Pour package of Jell-O over cottage cheese and mix well. Add pineapple and fold in Cool Whip.

2. Refrigerate until ready to serve. You can also add chopped walnuts or pecans if desired.

Cottage cheese will remain fresh for a longer time if you store it upside down in the refrigerator.

★ ★ ★ ★ ★ ★ ★ ★ ★ ★ ★ ★ ★ ★ ★ ★ ★ ★ ★ ★

JOHN WILLIAMS CONDUCTOR/COMPOSER

Whole-wheat Pancakes

1 EGG
1 CUP NONFAT PLAIN YOGURT
1 TABLESPOON BUTTER, MELTED
1 TABLESPOON MAPLE SYRUP
1 TEASPOON VANILLA
1 CUP WHOLE-WHEAT PASTRY FLOUR

1 TEASPOON BAKING POWDER
3/4 TEASPOON SALT (OR LESS)
1/2 TEASPOON BAKING SODA
NUTMEG (OPTIONAL)
NONFAT MILK

1. Combine egg, yogurt, butter, maple syrup, and vanilla in bowl and blend well.

2. Whisk in flour, baking powder, salt, baking soda, and nutmeg just until blended. Add just enough nonfat milk to achieve pancake batter consistency.

3. Drop by large spoonfuls into nonstick skillet and cook on both sides until golden.

Serves 2.

A good way to keep pancakes from sticking to the griddle is to fill a small piece of cheesecloth with salt, then rub the salt bag over the surface of the hot griddle just before pouring the batter.

OPRAH WINFREY

TELEVISION TALK SHOW HOST/ACTRESS

Oprah's Potatoes

2 1/2 POUNDS RED POTATOES
2 1/2 POUNDS IDAHO POTATOES
1/2 CUP BUTTER BUDS POWDER
1 CUP CHICKEN STOCK
2 CUPS NONFAT MILK

1/4 CUP CREAMED HORSERADISH
1/8 TEASPOON CAYENNE PEPPER
   (OPTIONAL)
1 1/2 TEASPOONS BLACK PEPPER

1. Scrub potatoes, leaving skin on; cut in half. Place potatoes in large pot and add water to cover. Bring to boil; reduce heat to low. Cover and simmer until potatoes are very tender.

2. Drain potatoes. Add Butter Buds and begin to mash. Add chicken stock, milk, horseradish, cayenne and black peppers and mash until potatoes are creamy but slightly lumpy.

Serves 12.

When choosing potatoes, look for ones that are smooth, well shaped, and unbruised. Do not buy if they have sprouted or have a green tint to the skin (this indicates a high solanine content). Store at room temperature in a dark area and do not refrigerate; refrigeration may turn a percentage of the starch into sugar.

KRISTI YAMAGUCHI

OLYMPIC CHAMPION — FIGURE SKATING

Sweet and Sour Chicken Wings

3 POUNDS CHICKEN WINGS
GARLIC SALT
3/4 CUP SUGAR
1/2 CUP VINEGAR
3 TO 4 TABLESPOONS KETCHUP

1 TABLESPOON SOY SAUCE
CORNSTARCH
2 EGGS, BEATEN
VEGETABLE OIL FOR DEEP FRYING

1. Cut chicken wings into sections. Sprinkle with garlic salt. Let stand 1 hour.

2. Combine sugar, vinegar, ketchup, and soy sauce in saucepan and heat until sugar dissolves. Set sweet and sour sauce aside.

3. Heat vegetable oil in pan to 375°F. Roll chicken pieces in cornstarch and dip in egg. Deep fry chicken in small batches being careful not to overcrowd pan. Fry until golden brown, about 5 minutes.

4. Preheat oven to 300°F. After all chicken has been fried, dip each piece in sweet and sour sauce. Arrange in shallow baking pan and bake 45 minutes.

Serves 6 to 8.

COOKING TERMS FROM A TO Z

AGE *To leave meat to hang, bringing out the flavor and tenderizing the meat.*

AL DENTE *Slightly underdone with a chewy consistency. Term usually applied to the cooking of pasta, but can also apply to vegetables that are blanched, not fully cooked.*

AU JUS *Roasted beef or lamb served with natural pan juices that accumulate during cooking.*

BAKE *To cook by free-circulating dry air. It is important to preheat an oven before putting in food. Do not crowd food in oven—give it room to cook evenly.*

BARBECUE *To cook meats, fish, and poultry over natural woods or charcoal on a grill, in open pits, or on a spit over intense heat, marinating first, then basting with a sauce.*

BARD *To cover meat entirely with a thin layer of fat to keep it from drying out during cooking.*

BASTE *To keep food moist during cooking by brushing, spooning, or drizzling with pan juice, sauce, or wine.*

BEAT *To mix ingredients rapidly so that air is incorporated, resulting in a smooth creamy mixture.*

BIND *To add an ingredient such as an egg, which holds the other ingredients together.*

BLANCH *To plunge vegetables, seafood, or fruit into boiling water for a brief period of time to bring out the color, loosen skins for peeling, or mellow flavors.*

BLEND *To combine ingredients together to a desired consistency, usually until smooth.*

BOIL *To heat water or other liquids to 212°F at sea level. When water boils, its surface is covered with bubbles.*

BONE *To remove the bones from fish, poultry, or meats, often with a boning knife.*

BRAISE *To brown meat in fat over high heat, then cover and cook slowly in the oven in a small amount of liquid.*

BREAD *To dredge or coat with bread crumbs such as fish dipped in milk, coated with crumbs, and baked or pan-fried.*

BROCHETTE *Meat, chicken, fish, or vegetables threaded on a skewer and then baked, broiled, or grilled.*

BROIL *To cook with intense heat either on a grill or under a broiler. The high heat seals in the juices, browns the outside, and keeps food moist and tender.*

BROWN *To cook food quickly in a preheated hot oven, broiler, or hot skillet to "brown" the outside and seal in the juices.*

BRUISE *To crush an aromatic food, such as garlic, to release flavor.*

CANDY *To cook and coat ingredients in a sugar syrup.*

CARAMELIZE *To dissolve sugar and water slowly, then heat until it turns caramel brown.*

CHIFFONADE *Very finely shredded or sliced leafy vegetables used as a garnish.*

CHOP *To cut food into pieces, which can range in size from finely chopped to coarsely chopped.*

CLARIFY *To clear stock by straining or to make butter clear by heating, separating, and discarding milk solids.*

CODDLE *To poach in slowly simmering water, as a coddled egg.*

CRACKLINGS *The crisp brown bits that remain when all the fat is rendered from chicken and duck skin or from pork rinds.*

CREAM *To mix a softened ingredient, like butter, alone or with other ingredients, such as sugar, until well blended and completely soft.*

CRIMP To decorate the edge of a pie crust by pinching dough together with fingers.

CUBE To cut food into square-shaped pieces, ranging in size from 1/4 inch to 1 inch.

CURDLE The separation that occurs in egg- or cream-based mixtures when they are heated too quickly.

CURE To preserve meats by either drying, pickling, salting, or smoking.

CUT To combine butter or vegetable shortening with dry ingredients, using a pastry blender or the fingers, until the mixture resembles coarse meal.

DASH A small quantity.

DEGLAZE To add broth, water, or wine to a pan in which food, usually meat or poultry, has been cooked, stirring and scraping up and dissolving the browned bits from the bottom of the pan. Once the food has been cooked, remove it from the pan, add the liquid, and heat; stir the juices and scrape the bits remaining in the pan until the liquid is reduced to the desired consistency.

DEGREASE To carefully skim the layer of fat from the top of a sauce, soup, or stock.

DEVEIN To remove the intestinal tract of a shrimp. After a shrimp has been shelled, make a slit lengthwise on the outermost curve with a knife and remove the intestinal tract. Rinse under cold water.

DEVIL To mix cooked chopped foods into a sauce of wine or vinegar that has been spiced with a combination of hot ingredients such as dry mustard, paprika, or Tabasco.

DICE To cut into equal-size small cubes from 1/4 to 1/2 inch.

DILUTE To make a sauce or stock less strong by adding additional liquid.

DOT To scatter small pieces of butter, usually about 1/4-inch square, over the top layer of a prepared dish.

DRAIN To remove liquid or fat from food through a strainer or by absorption on a towel.

DREDGE To lightly coat food, usually with bread crumbs or flour. Fill a paper or plastic bag with flour, spices, and ingredients to be cooked. Shake the mixture, and shake off excess before browning.

DRIPPINGS The juices, fat, and brown bits that are left in a pan after poultry or meat has been roasted or sautéed. After fat has been skimmed, the drippings are often used for gravies and sauces.

DRIZZLE To slowly pour a very thin stream of liquid lightly over food.

FILLET To cut meat, chicken, or fish from the bones.

FLAKE To test the flesh of fish to see if it is done by lightly breaking away a small piece with a fork.

FOLD To incorporate one ingredient into another without stirring or beating, but instead by gently lifting from underneath with a rubber spatula.

FRY To cook food in hot fat in a skillet over high heat until brown and crisp. Foods to be fried are often dipped in batter or flour first.

GARNISH To decorate food with fresh herbs, fresh vegetables, edible flowers, or fruit to enhance the presentation of the dish.

GRATE To change a solid food into fine shreds by rubbing it against a hand grater or placing it in a food processor.

GREASE To lightly coat a pan with oil or fat to prevent foods from sticking and to help in browning.

GRILL To cook on a rack over very hot coals or under a broiler in order to seal in juices.

GRIND To use a mortar and pestle, a food processor, or a meat grinder to transform a solid piece of food into fine pieces.

HULL To pluck out the green stems and leaves of berries.

HUSK To remove the outside leaves from an ear of corn.

JULIENNE To cut fresh vegetables or other food into thin, match-size strips of uniform length.

KNEAD *To work dough, after blending ingredients, with the palms of your hands on a lightly floured surface, making the dough smooth and elastic.*

LEAVEN *To cause a mixture to rise while it is baking by adding baking powder, baking soda, or yeast.*

LINE *To cover the surface of a baking sheet or roasting pan with parchment or waxed paper to prevent food from sticking.*

MACERATE *To cover fruits or vegetables with a liquid, often liqueur or lemon juice and sugar, and let it rest until the flavor has been absorbed and the fruits or vegetables have softened.*

MARINATE *To tenderize and flavor food by placing it in a seasoned liquid, usually composed of some combination of vinegar, lemon juice, wine, oil, herbs, and/or spices.*

MELT *To change solids into liquids by use of slow heat.*

MINCE *To cut or chop into very fine pieces, not larger than 1/8-inch square.*

MIX *To stir ingredients together with a fork or spoon.*

MULL *To infuse hot cider or wine with herbs and spices.*

PAN-BROIL *To cook on top of the stove in a preheated heavy skillet over high heat, pouring off fat or liquid as it accumulates.*

PARBOIL *To partially cook in boiling water or broth. Often vegetables are parboiled and finished off with a quick sauté.*

PARE *To use a thin knife to remove rind or skin from fruits and vegetables.*

PINCH *The amount of a dry ingredient you can hold between your thumb and finger.*

PIT *To remove the pits from fruit.*

PLUMP *To soak dried fruits in liquid until they swell and are rehydrated.*

POACH *To cook food gently in simmering liquid that does not boil.*

POUND *To flatten or tenderize meat, often between sheets of waxed paper, with a heavy mallet.*

PREHEAT *To set an oven or broiler at the desired cooking temperature 15 to 30 minutes before use so that the desired temperature is reached before food is placed in to cook.*

PRICK *To pierce food or pastry with the tines of a fork to prevent it from bursting or rising during baking.*

PROOF *To test yeast to see if it is active. Dissolve yeast in warm water mixed with a little sugar. Let stand in a warm place for 5 to 10 minutes. If the yeast is active, it will bubble and foam.*

PUREE *To mash solid food or pass it through a food mill or food processor until it is smooth.*

RECONSTITUTE *To rehydrate dry food by soaking in liquid.*

REDUCE *To thicken or concentrate a sauce by boiling down, which lessens the volume and intensifies the flavor.*

REFRESH *To run hot vegetables under cold water or to plunge them into cold water to stop the cooking process and retain color.*

RENDER *To liquefy a solid fat over low heat.*

RICE *To push a soft, cooked food such as potatoes through a mesh strainer or a potato ricer.*

ROAST *To cook by the free circulation of dry heat, often beginning with a very hot oven to seal in juices and then lowering the heat to complete the cooking.*

ROUX *A mixture of melted butter and flour cooked over low heat to make a base for thickening sauce.*

SAUTÉ *To cook food in butter or fat in a skillet until lightly browned.*

SCALD *To cook a liquid, most often milk or cream, over low heat until just before it boils.*

SCORE To make very thin slashes along the surface of fish or meat to help tenderize it.

SEAR To brown the surface of meat very quickly in a hot oven, under a broiler, or in a pan over high heat on top of the stove to seal in juices.

SHRED To tear or cut into long, thin pieces.

SIFT To pass dry ingredients, most often flour, through a fine-mesh strainer to remove lumps and lighten the texture.

SIMMER To cook liquid alone or along with other ingredients over low heat, never boiling.

SKIM To spoon off fat or scum that rises to the surface of a cooked liquid.

SLIVER To cut food into long, thin strips.

SNIP To cut herbs such as chives into small bits with scissors.

SPIT-ROAST To cook meats, often whole meats, on a metal rod rotating over a hot fire.

STEAM To cook food, covered, over a small amount of boiling water. Great low-fat method of cooking, especially good for vegetables.

STEEP To place dry ingredients such as tea leaves into warm liquid to infuse the liquid with flavor and color.

STEW To slowly cook meats and vegetables in liquid in a covered pan, either on top of the stove or in the oven.

STIR To blend a mixture together using a spoon in a circular motion.

STIR-FRY To quickly sauté meat or vegetables while stirring constantly in a hot wok or skillet.

STOCK A long-simmering, well-flavored broth made from fish, poultry, meat, or vegetables with the addition of herbs and spices.

STRAIN To remove solids from liquids by pouring through a colander or sieve.

STUD To insert seasonings such as garlic or whole cloves into the surface of a food to infuse it with flavor.

STUFF To fill a cavity with a well-flavored mixture. Let stuffing come to room temperature before using it and stuff meats, poultry, and fish just before cooking.

TEMPER To moderate and balance a cool ingredient before gradually adding it to a hot ingredient, or vice versa, to avoid separation and curdling.

TOAST To brown by baking, such as seeds and nuts, or to brown by placing food under direct heat.

TOSS To quickly and gently mix ingredients together using a large fork or spoon.

TRUSS To tie the legs and wings of poultry close to the body with string in preparation for roasting.

VINAIGRETTE A dressing made from a mixture of vinegar, oil, salt, and pepper. Mustard, herbs, garlic, or shallots may also be added. Use as a salad dressing.

WHIP To beat rapidly, either by hand or with an electric mixer, to add air and increase volume.

ZEST To remove in fine strips the outermost colored peel, or zest, of citrus fruits, being careful not to incorporate the bitter white pith just underneath the surface.

GLOSSARY OF HERBS AND SPICES

ALLSPICE *A pea-size fruit that grows in Mexico, Jamaica, and South America. Allspice tastes like a blend of cinnamon, cloves, and nutmeg. Excellent in spice cakes and cookies, apple and peach pies, steamed puddings, fruit preserves, and relishes.*

ANCHO CHILI PEPPER *Large, juicy, dark purple New Mexican pods. Most commonly used pepper in Mexico in such traditional dishes as red chili and tamales.*

ANISE *Small, licorice-flavored seeds. Great in breads, cakes, and cookies.*

ANNATTO SEEDS *A must for South American, Caribbean, Mexican, and Spanish cooking. Use to impart red color and pungent flavor to rice or polenta, for frying chicken or fish, and braising pork or beef for enchiladas.*

ARROWROOT STARCH *Arrowroot has long been used in making clear glazes for fruit pies or Chinese clear gravies. Because of its superior thickening ability and clear finish, it is excellent for thickening the sauce for stir-fried seafood and poultry dishes.*

BASIL *Herb with an aromatic, leafy flavor. Grown in the United States and North Mediterranean area. Varieties include sweet basil, dark opal, and lemon basil. Use with pasta, poultry, fish, eggs, and tomato dishes.*

BAY LEAF *Pungent herb with sturdy leaves and faint cinnamon taste grown in the eastern Mediterranean countries. A must for bouquet garni and pickling. Good in meat, stews, soups, and bean dishes.*

CARAWAY *Nutty, licorice-flavored seeds grown in the Netherlands. Use with eggs, cheese spreads, and dips; rye bread; cole slaw; and with vegetables such as beets, cabbage, potatoes, turnips, and squash.*

CARDAMOM *Fragrant cinnamon-like seed popular in Indian dishes and baked goods. Use in spice cakes and cookies, apple and pumpkin pies, and curries.*

CAYENNE *Red pepper of the capsicum family most often used dried. Add to dishes if you want a little heat!*

CELERY SEEDS *Dried seed tasting strongly of celery. Great in potato, cole slaw, and vegetable salads.*

CHERVIL *Herb with a subtle, celery-licorice taste. Use in green salads; with fish, shellfish, and chicken. Try with tomatoes or string beans.*

CHILI POWDER *A mix of ground chili peppers, cumin, oregano, and other herbs and spices. A must for chili!*

CHIPOTLE PEPPERS *Ripe, red jalapeño pepper that has been slowly wood-smoked. They are rich, smoky, and hot. Used in chili, tomato sauce, stew, beans, and rice dishes.*

CHIVE *Herb with light onion or garlic taste. Good with fish, shellfish, cream sauces, and soups.*

CINNAMON *Spice bark of the cassia tree, sweet hot flavor. Use in spice cakes, cookies, pumpkin pie; sprinkle on carrots, winter squash, and sweet potatoes.*

CLOVE *Pungent and sweet spice. Spike a ham with whole cloves; add ground cloves to cakes, cookies, and fruit pies.*

COCOA *There are two types: Natural cocoa is strong, dark, and bittersweet—perfect for baking; Dutch cocoa is processed to temper the natural acidity of the cocoa bean, yielding a smooth, rich, and slightly less strong cocoa that mixes more freely in liquid. Great for hot chocolate and flavored coffee.*

CORIANDER/CILANTRO *Nutty-tasting seeds are called coriander. Cilantro is the herb.*

Use whole seeds for pickles and ground for baking. Cilantro is the essential herb for Latin, Mexican, and Asian cooking. Use with fish, shellfish, poultry, salsas, and salads.

CREAM OF TARTAR Used to stabilize delicate foods like meringue toppings and other baked egg-white dishes.

CRUSHED RED PEPPERS Hot chili peppers are used whole in many Asian countries. Great for pizza, tacos, spaghetti, omelets, and beans.

CUMIN A small, hot, bitter seed. Essential spice for curry and chili powder. Excellent with curried vegetables, fish, lamb, and poultry.

CURRY POWDER A ground blend of ginger, turmeric, fenugreek seeds, as many as 16 to 20 spices. For all Indian curry recipes such as lamb, chicken, beef, rice, and vegetables.

DILL Herb and seeds have a delicate caraway taste. Use both seeds and herb for making pickles. Dill adds pleasing flavor to sauerkraut and potato salad. Fresh dill is good with seafood and chicken.

FENNEL SEEDS Slight licorice flavor, similar to anise and dill. Used in Scandinavian breads, cakes, and cookies. Also good with vegetables, in salads, and salad dressings.

GARLIC Probably the most heavily used seasoning in the world. All the world's great cuisines, from Chinese to Italian to French, make abundant use of this pungent flavoring.

GINGER Widely used spice with aroma and bite. Use ground dried in cakes, cookies, pumpkin pie, custard, and marinades. Use fresh grated or sliced in marinades and stir-fries. Crystallized and preserved ginger is great in cakes and cookies.

JUNIPER Strong spiceberry mostly used in making gin. Can be used in marinades for beef, fish, poultry, and pork.

LAVENDER Herb with a fresh, clean scent. Add to fruit, iced tea, or herbs de Provence.

LEMON GRASS A straw-like stalk with a woodsy, lemony flavor. Used in Near Eastern and Indonesian cooking. Try it with chicken, fish, and shellfish.

LEMON PEEL Zest from outer peel has excellent flavor and bright, yellow color. Used in muffins, cookies, cakes, and many other dishes.

MACE Outer covering of nutmeg; flavor similar to but milder than nutmeg. For pickling, fish, stewed fruit; delicious in baked goods, pastries, and doughnuts.

MARJORAM Herb that is first cousin to oregano with similar but more delicate taste. Grown in France and Chile. Use with fish, meat, poultry, and in vegetable dishes, soups, and stews.

MINT Refreshing herb with cool taste and scent. There are over 30 varieties, but peppermint and spearmint are the best known. Use in Middle Eastern cooking such as tabbouleh. Great in salads, desserts, and iced tea.

NUTMEG Sweet, nutty spice from the nutmeg tree. Excellent in cakes, cookies, pastries, pies, custard, and eggnog. Try in cream sauces and soups.

OREGANO Herb with pungent marjoram taste. Essential for Italian, Greek, and Mexican cooking. Use with poultry, fish, meat, and vegetables.

PAPRIKA Ground spice of dried capsicum peppers grown in Spain, Central Europe, and the United States. A must for goulash and paprikash. Good in dips, salad dressings, and with fish, poultry, and shellfish.

PARSLEY Two common varieties—Italian flat leaf and curly leaf—the flat leaf has a stronger flavor. Curly parsley is used for garnishing. Use in soups, stocks, tomato sauces, salads, and salad dressings; and with fish, poultry, and vegetables.

POPPY SEEDS Very tiny, blue-black seeds of the poppy flower. It takes 900,000 seeds to make a pound! Use for cakes, cookies, pastries, and breads.

ROSEMARY Needle-like leaves with a strong, piney scent and flavor. Grown in France, Spain, and Portugal. Excellent with poultry, meats, and game; and with oven-roasted potatoes.

SAFFRON Expensive, fragrant spice that is the dried stigmas of crocus. A little goes a long way. Use in bouillabaisse, paella, risotto, and cream soups.

SAGE Herb with a musky flavor grown in Greece, Yugoslavia, and Albania. Excellent for poultry stuffing. Use with chicken, duck, goose, pork, turkey, sausages, meatloaf, and stews.

SAVORY Peppery herb that has two varieties — summer and winter. Summer savory is best for cooking, great in meatloaf and meatballs; and with lima beans, string beans, lentils, and dried beans.

TARRAGON Herb with a mild, licorice flavor. Use with chicken, fish, shellfish, veal, eggs; and in salad dressings and mayonnaise.

THYME Herb with tiny leaves and minty, tea-like flavor. Varieties include lemon, orange, English, and French thyme. Use with fish, sausages, pates, and stuffings. Excellent with poultry, beans, eggplant, tomatoes, and potatoes.

TURMERIC A root of the ginger family, grown in India, Haiti, Jamaica, and Peru. Brilliant yellow ground spice. Essential to curry powder, mustard, pickles, and relish.

★ ★ ★ ★ ★ ★ ★ ★ ★ ★ ★ ★ ★ ★ ★ ★ ★ ★ ★

INDEX OF RECIPE TITLES

★

RECIPE INDEX

★ ★ ★ ★ ★ ★ ★ ★ ★ ★ ★ ★ ★ ★ ★ ★ ★ ★ ★ ★

Muskingum Chocolate Dew Cake, 68

Potato Cake with a Chicory-chocolate
  Chantilly, 26

Strawberry Cheesecake, 49

Strawberry Shortcake, 67

CANDIES, ETC.

Caramel Corn, 115

Peanut Butter Fudge, 62

COOKIES

Brownie Meringues, 50

Chocolate Chip Cookies, 35

Lace Cookies, 76

Lemon Loves, 38

Peanut Butter Cookies, 24

CUSTARDS, PUDDINGS, MOUSSE

Amaretto Caramel Custard, 108

Buzz's Quick 'n Easy Chocolate Mousse, 12

Custard Rice Pudding, 47

Mouthwatering Bread Pudding, 36

DESSERT FROSTINGS,
FILLINGS, ETC.

Blueberry Filling, 30

Cherry Filling, 30

Chocolate Glaze, 71

Coca-Cola Topping, 58

PIES, TARTS, ETC.

Abby's Famous Pecan Pie, 125

Caramelized Lemon Tart, 52

Noodle Kugel, 92

Red, White, and Blue Cobbler, 30

Rustic Apple Tart, 59

Sliced Peach Betty, 20

INDEX OF CELEBRITIES

★ ★ ★ ★ ★ ★ ★ ★ ★ ★ ★ ★ ★ ★ ★ ★ ★ ★ ★ ★